The Scopes Trial

by Don Nardo

FAMOUS TRIALS

Lucent Books, San Diego, CA

Other books in the Famous Trials series:

The Dred Scott Decision
The Nuremberg Trials
The O.J. Simpson Trial
The Salem Witch Trials
The Trial of Socrates

Library of Congress Cataloging-in-Publication Data
Nardo, Don, 1947–
   The Scopes trial / by Don Nardo.
      p. cm. — (Famous trials)
   Includes bibliographical references and index.
   Summary: Examines the Scopes trial concerning the teaching of evolution in public schools.
   ISBN 1-56006-268-1 (alk. paper)
   1. Scopes, John Thomas—Trials, litigation, etc.—Juvenile literature. 2. Evolution—Study and teaching—Law and legislation—Tennessee—Juvenile literature. [1. Scopes, John Thomas—Trials, litigation, etc. 2. Evolution—Study and teaching—Law and legislation.] I. Title. II. Series: Famous trials series.
KF224.S3N37   1997
345.73'0288
[347.305288]—DC20   96-34421
                                   CIP
                                   AC

Table of Contents

Foreword

"The law is not an end in and of itself, nor does it provide ends. It is preeminently a means to serve what we think is right."

William J. Brennan Jr.

THE CONCEPT OF JUSTICE AND THE RULE OF LAW are hallmarks of Western civilization, manifested perhaps most visibly in widely famous and dramatic court trials. These trials include such important and memorable personages as the ancient Greek philosopher Socrates, who was accused and convicted of corrupting the minds of his society's youth in 399 B.C.; the French maiden and military leader Joan of Arc, accused and convicted of heresy against the church in 1431; and former football star O. J. Simpson, acquitted of double murder in 1995. These and other well-known and controversial trials constitute the most public, and therefore most familiar, demonstrations of a Western legal tradition that dates back through the ages. Although no one is certain when the first law code appeared or when the first formal court trials were held, Babylonian ruler Hammurabi introduced the first known law code in about 1760 B.C. It remains unclear how this code was administered, and no records of specific trials have survived. What is clear, however, is that humans have always sought to govern behavior and define actions in terms of law.

Almost all societies have made laws and prosecuted people for going against those laws, but the question of which behaviors to sanction and which to censure has always been controversial and remains in flux. Some, such as Roman orator and legislator Cicero, argue that laws are simply applications of universal standards. Cicero believed that humanity would agree on what constituted illegal behavior and that human laws were a mere extension of natural laws. "True law is right reason in agreement with nature," he wrote,

5

world-wide in scope, unchanging, everlasting. . . . We may not oppose or alter that law, we cannot abolish it, we cannot be freed from its obligations by any legislature. . . .This [natural] law does not differ for Rome and for Athens, for the present and for the future. . . . It is and will be valid for all nations and all times.

Cicero's rather optimistic view has been contradicted throughout history, however. For every law made to preserve harmony and set universal standards of behavior, another has been born of fear, prejudice, greed, desire for power, and a host of other motives. History is replete with individuals defying and fighting to change such laws—and even to topple governments that dictate such laws. Abolitionists fought against slavery, civil rights leaders fought for equal rights, millions throughout the world have fought for independence—these constitute a minimum of reasons for which people have sought to overturn laws that they believed to be wrong or unjust. In opposition to Cicero, then, many others, such as eighteenth-century English poet and philosopher William Godwin, believe humans must be constantly vigilant against bad laws. As Godwin said in 1793:

Laws we sometimes call the wisdom of our ancestors. But this is a strange imposition. It was as frequently the dictate of their passion, of timidity, jealousy, a monopolizing spirit, and a lust of power that knew no bounds. Are we not obliged perpetually to renew and remodel this misnamed wisdom of our ancestors? To correct it by a detection of their ignorance, and a censure of their intolerance?

Lucent Books' *Famous Trials* series showcases trials that exemplify both society's praiseworthy condemnation of universally unacceptable behavior, and its misguided persecution of individuals based on fear and ignorance, as well as trials that leave open the question of whether justice has been done. Each volume begins by setting the scene and providing a historical context to show how society's mores influence the trial process and the verdict. Each book goes on to present a detailed and lively account of the trial, including liberal use of primary source material such as direct testimony, lawyers' summations, and contemporary and modern commentary. In addition, sidebars throughout the text create a broader context by presenting illuminating details about important points of law, information on key personalities, and important distinctions related to civil, federal, and criminal procedures. Thus, all of the primary and secondary source material included in both the text and the sidebars demonstrates to readers the sources and methods historians use to derive information and conclusions about such events.

Lastly, each *Famous Trials* volume includes one or more of the following comprehensive tools that motivate readers to pursue further reading and research. A timeline allows readers to see the scope of the trial at a glance, annotated bibliographies provide both sources for further research and a thorough list of works consulted, a glossary helps students with unfamiliar words and concepts, and a comprehensive index permits quick scanning of the book as a whole.

The insight of Oliver Wendell Holmes Jr., distinguished Supreme Court justice, exemplifies the theme of the *Famous Trials* series. Taken from *The Common Law*, published in 1881, Holmes remarked: "The life of the law has not been logic, it has been experience." That "experience" consists mainly in how laws are applied in society and challenged in the courts, a process resulting in differing outcomes from one generation to the next. Thus, the *Famous Trials* series encourages readers to examine trials within a broader historical and social context.

Introduction

Six Days or Forever?

BEADS OF PERSPIRATION FORMED on the bald pate of the portly man in the witness chair. Sixty-five-year-old William Jennings Bryan, golden-throated orator, former U. S. secretary of state, and three-time national presidential candidate, was known as the Great Commoner because he had long championed the interests of everyday American workers against big business. Often, he toured the country, speaking to legions of adoring fans at political rallies and religious revival or "tent" meetings. Now, on this July day in 1925, he sat, sweating profusely in nearly one-hundred-degree heat, on the front lawn of the courthouse in the tiny rural town of Dayton, Tennessee.

Bryan had volunteered to lead local prosecutors in trying a Dayton high school teacher, John T. Scopes, who stood accused of breaking a new state law. This law forbade the teaching of Charles Darwin's theory of evolution, which holds that all living things, including humans, descended from lower life-forms. Like many other Americans, Bryan was disturbed that such a "god-less" idea was commonly taught in most American biology classes. He saw evolution, which he called the "brute theory," as dangerous because it might make children "lose the conscious-ness of God's presence in our daily life." In his view, the events described in Genesis, the first book of the Bible, constituted the one true version of creation and this was what schools should be teaching. "You may trace your ancestry back to the monkey if you find pleasure or pride in doing so," he had declared on more than one occasion, "but you shall not connect me with your family tree without more evidence than has yet been produced." It was this firm antievolution stance that had made Bryan the logical choice to come to Dayton and set an example for other "modernists" and "atheists" who might try to subvert and degrade wholesome American values and traditions.

William Jennings Bryan, dubbed the Great Commoner, was the head prosecutor during the Scopes trial.

All present at the Dayton courthouse that day were surprised to see Bryan testifying because it was, and still is, unusual for the head prosecutor in a trial to be called as a witness. This legal ploy, which would soon prove to be a brilliant and devastating maneuver, was the work of Scopes's chief defense counsel, sixty-eight-year-old Clarence Darrow, at the time the most famous trial lawyer in the United States. Darrow had come to Dayton with the same zeal and sense of purpose that had animated Bryan. "For the first, the last, the only time in my life," Darrow would later recall,

> I volunteered my services in a case . . . because I really wanted to take part in it. . . . An organization calling themselves "fundamentalists" had been very actively seeking to control the schools and universities of America. The members of this body claimed to believe that the . . . Bible . . . was virtually written by the Almighty and is in every part literally true. . . . [Legislative] bills were prepared to forbid the teaching of evolution, or any doctrine in conflict with the Genesis story, in any school wholly or in part supported by public funds. . . . I was in New York not long after the arrest of Mr. Scopes, and saw that Mr. Bryan had volunteered to go to Dayton to assist in the prosecution. At once I wanted to go. My object, and my only object, was to focus the attention of the country on the program of Mr. Bryan and the other fundamentalists in America. I knew that education was in danger from the source that has always hampered it—religious fanaticism.

Indeed, exposing the fundamentalists' leading spokesman as a fanatic who refused even to consider the worth of nonbiblical explanations of creation had been Darrow's strategy in putting Bryan on the stand. "Do you claim that everything in the Bible should be literally interpreted?" Darrow asked, leaning toward his opponent in the witness box.

"I believe that everything in the Bible should be accepted as it is given there," Bryan declared proudly.

"When you read that the whale swallowed Jonah, how do you literally interpret that?"

"When I read that a big fish swallowed Jonah, I believe it, and I believe in a god who can make a whale and can make a man and make them both do what he pleases." The Commoner fanned himself, grinned, and forcefully added, "One miracle is just as easy to believe as another."

Famed lawyer Clarence Darrow defended John T. Scopes in a test case to challenge the Butler Act.

Bryan maintained this confident air for a while; but after more than an hour of Darrow's relentless grilling under the merciless midday sun, the witness began to lose his composure. Barraged by question after pointed question about why so many biblical claims seemed to go against scientific evidence and just plain common sense, Bryan seemed increasingly confused and unsure.

Finally, the wily Darrow asked, "Do you think the earth was made in six days?" The content of this question seemed concisely to symbolize the controversy that lay at the heart of the Scopes trial. Should people blindly accept the statement in the Bible that God had created the heavens, the earth, and the plants and animals in the brief span of six days? Or should they trust the overwhelming scientific evidence that the earth's formation and the evolution of its life-forms had taken many millions of years? As historian Ray Ginger later aptly summed it up, Had the whole majestic process taken six days or, in a sense, forever? Bryan's surprising answer to this simple yet profound question posed by Darrow would not only surprise and electrify both the members of the court audience and millions of other people worldwide, but would also shape the course of the Bible/evolution debate for years to come.

Chapter 1

Natural Selection Versus Original Sin: The Roots of Evolution and Antievolution

THE DISPUTE OVER THE TEACHING of evolution in public schools, which spawned the world-famous Scopes Monkey Trial in Tennessee in 1925, was part of a larger debate between the forces of science and religion that began in the 1860s. Late in 1859, English naturalist Charles Darwin published his *On the Origin of Species By Means of Natural Selection*, a massive collection of scientific evidence supporting the theory of evolution. Scientists and also many educated nonscientists, including many religious leaders, soon came to accept Darwin's thesis. But those who held that the Bible is the revealed word of God, and therefore that its contents are literal fact, refused to accept any idea or claim that contradicted the biblical explanation for the creation of the world. In time, as the theory of evolution became part of the regular curriculum of biology classes around the United States, the religious fundamentalists began to feel threatened. They feared that learning about evolution might confuse, twist, and corrupt their children's minds and cause them to turn away from religion and its moral teachings; and this fear was what eventually led to Tennessee's law forbidding the teaching of evolution and to the arrest of John Scopes.

A Fierce Struggle for Existence

At first, the biblical literalists were not the only ones who objected to Darwin's ideas. Immediately after the first print run of the *Origin of Species* appeared in November 1859, a heated controversy erupted in which many prominent scholars and clergymen publicly attacked Darwin and his book. One religious leader called him "the most dangerous man in England." The well-known geologist Adam Sedgwick, who had once been Darwin's teacher and friend, described whole sections of the book as "utterly false and grievously mischievous." Darwin's theory, said Sedgwick, was sure to "sink the human race into a lower grade of degradation than any into which it has fallen since its written record tells us of its history."

Charles Darwin's book Origin of Species *created a great deal of controversy for its revolutionary ideas.*

It is important to note that all this fuss about Darwin supposedly degrading humanity resulted more from what some people inferred from the book than from what he actually wrote. The *Origin of Species* does not deal directly with human evolution from more primitive creatures; Darwin reserved that subject for his 1871 book, *The Descent of Man.* The first book was primarily an introduction to the concept of natural selection, which, he asserted, helped to drive the process of evolution. According to Darwin, physical characteristics such as size, strength, shape of body parts, and quality of vision and hearing regularly pass from parents to offspring. This process is random, however, and always results in tiny variations from one generation to another. Also, he explained, life consists of a fierce struggle for existence in which creatures of all species compete for the same limited supplies of food, water, and territory. Darwin wrote that this struggle "will be most

ON

THE ORIGIN OF SPECIES

BY MEANS OF NATURAL SELECTION,

OR THE

PRESERVATION OF FAVOURED RACES IN THE STRUGGLE
FOR LIFE.

BY CHARLES DARWIN, M.A.,
FELLOW OF THE ROYAL, GEOLOGICAL, LINNÆAN, ETC., SOCIETIES;
AUTHOR OF 'JOURNAL OF RESEARCHES DURING H. M. S. BEAGLE'S VOYAGE
ROUND THE WORLD.'

LONDON:
JOHN MURRAY, ALBEMARLE STREET.
1859.

The right of Translation is reserved.

The title page of the book that caused such public furor.

severe between the individuals of the same species, for they frequent the same districts, require the same food, and are exposed to the same dangers."

Following from these facts, Darwin's essential thesis was that nature tends to "select," or allow the survival of, those individuals whose variations are favored over those of others; that is, plants and animals that manage to adapt to changing environmental conditions will survive and pass on their favorable characteristics to their offspring. These new, favored kinds of living things will, over time, become increasingly different from their original parents, and after the passage of thousands of generations they will have become different enough to constitute a new species. At the same time, Darwin observed, species with favored characteristics tend to crowd out those that cannot adapt as quickly or as well. These less successful living things inevitably become extinct. Thus, he said, although evolution occurs much too slowly to be directly detectable, its workings can be seen in the fossil record, which reveals the rise and fall of countless species over the eons. Darwin's thesis neatly explained why the most ancient fossils least

DARWIN'S "LOAD OF PREJUDICE"

In the conclusion of his landmark book, *Origin of Species*, Darwin, who fully anticipated strong objections from all quarters, included this appeal to the common sense and fairness of religious leaders and scientists alike:

I see no good reason why the views given in this volume should shock the religious feelings of any one. It is satisfactory, as showing how transient [temporary] such impressions are, to remember that the greatest discovery ever made by man, namely, the law of the attraction of gravity [by English scientist Isaac Newton], was also attacked . . . "as subversive of natural, and . . . revealed, religion." A celebrated author . . . has written to me that "he has gradually learnt to see that it is just as noble a conception of the Deity [God] to believe that He created a few original forms capable of self-development into other and needful forms, as to believe that He required a fresh act of creation to supply the voids caused by the action of His laws." Why, it may be asked, until recently did nearly all the most eminent living naturalists and geologists disbelieve in the mutability [capacity for change] of species? . . . The belief that species were immutable productions was almost unavoidable as long as the history of the world was thought to be of short duration. . . . But the chief cause of our natural unwillingness to admit that one species has given birth to clear and distinct species, is that we are always slow in admitting great changes of which we do not see the steps. . . . The mind cannot possibly grasp the full meaning of the term of even a million years; it cannot add up and perceive the full effects of many slight variations, accumulated during an almost infinite number of generations. Although I am fully convinced of the truth of the views given in this volume . . . I by no means expect to convince experienced naturalists whose . . . [views are] directly opposite to mine. . . . A few naturalists, endowed with much flexibility of mind, and who have already begun to doubt the immutability of species, may be influenced by this volume; but I look with confidence to the future,—to young and rising naturalists, who will be able to view both sides of the question with impartiality . . . for thus only can the load of prejudice by which this subject is overwhelmed be removed.

resemble modern ones. Succeeding generations of offspring become increasingly less like an original set of parents, and the longer evolution proceeds, the less the older forms resemble the new ones.

The Force of Truth and Fact

The idea that all the earth's life-forms have been and remain locked in an eternal, violent struggle in which the strong survive and the weak die out disturbed many people of Darwin's time. They, like nearly everyone before them, assumed that God had created all species miraculously, by decree, and that the forms of these plants and animals were immutable, or unchanging. Because they could not see the alleged process of evolution happening before their eyes, at first many people criticized Darwin and rejected his theory.

But despite the numerous assaults on his work and character, some of them quite vicious, Darwin prevailed. This was because the evidence he presented for the workings of the evolutionary process was overwhelming. In page after page, chapter after chapter, he had constructed a powerfully convincing case for natural selection. Near the end of the book, Darwin stated that no false theory could possibly explain so much so well; and indeed, as scholar Tom McGowen explains:

> It is a common happening in science that any theory based on incorrectly understood evidence or faulty reasoning eventually gets demolished by the work of other scientists, whereas a theory based fully on fact gains strength as new evidence comes to light, as was the case with [Polish astronomer Nicolaus] Copernicus' theory that the earth revolved around the sun. And even as the arguments about evolution were going on, new evidence was accumulating to back up Darwin's theory. . . . The discovery in 1856 of fossil skeletons of an apparently different human species [the Neanderthals] . . . showed that there had indeed been a more primitive kind of human. And the discovery of the fossil remains of a prehistoric creature that was clearly a combination of both reptile and bird [the archaeopteryx] . . . was a titanic piece of proof for Darwin's claim that birds had evolved from reptiles.

Darwin's book seemed to explain so much, so well about plants and animals that it quickly won the acceptance and strong support of several of the world's most renowned scientists. Among the first of these giants to champion Darwin were botanist Joseph Hooker, geologist Charles Lyell, and biologist Thomas Henry Huxley. As the book sold out in printing after printing, increasing numbers of scholars and other educated people found Darwin's arguments compelling and inescapable. So powerful were these arguments, in fact, that only four years after their publication nearly every important scientist in the world had accepted them. In 1863 Darwin's friend Reverend Charles Kingsley wrote to a friend, "Darwin is conquering everywhere and rushing in like a flood, by the mere force of truth and fact."

In the succeeding decades, even many religious leaders came to accept Darwin's ideas about evolution. A number of respected nineteenth-century biblical scholars studied earlier, non-English translations of the Bible, as well as the cultures of the peoples who lived in the ancient lands described in that book. These researches made it clear that the Old Testament had been produced over a span of several hundred years by a variety of authors. Moreover, many biblical stories had been based on or influenced by the legends of Middle Eastern peoples such as the Babylonians, suggesting that at least some of the Bible had to be regarded as fable or allegory. As a result, numerous religious leaders tried to reconcile the Bible with new and widely accepted scientific discoveries; for example, one increasingly popular view was that evolution was God's grand design for a kind of "ongoing" creation. This merging of religious and scientific ideas became known as religious "modernism."

The Rise of Fundamentalism

In time, it indeed seemed as if Darwin had "conquered everywhere." By 1900, four decades after he had published *Origin of Species*, the great controversy he had ignited had largely died down. Many biology textbooks routinely included sections on evolution and those that did not rapidly became outdated. This trend continued and accelerated until, by 1920, nearly every college and

Charles Darwin (left) and a manuscript page from Origin of Species. *Although controversial at first, Darwin's ideas gained acceptance among the general public and scientists alike.*

high school in Europe and the United States taught evolution in biology classes.

But as it turned out, the controversy about evolution and religion was far from over. All through the late 1800s and early 1900s, the fundamentalists, primarily Americans who lived in the rural South (the so-called "Bible belt"), remained outside the intellectual mainstream of the major organized religions by refusing to accept Darwin's ideas. They got their name from a series of ten pamphlets, titled *The Fundamentals*, that appeared in 1910. These writings, which circulated throughout the United States in the following years, were a reaction by very conservative biblical literalists to what they saw as a steady erosion of traditional faith in the Bible in favor of "godless" science. *The Fundamentals* tried to redefine what it meant to be a Christian, stressing the "Five Points" of true belief. These were the complete infallibility of the Bible; the virgin birth of Jesus Christ; Christ's voluntary death to atone for humanity's sins; Christ's resurrection into Heaven; and the authenticity of all miracles described in the Bible.

This conservative and rigid religious doctrine appealed to a growing number of people, and the fundamentalist movement rapidly gained steam in the United States and Canada. At first, small fundamentalist factions grew within established religious denominations such as the Methodists and Baptists. Later, after an interdenominational fundamentalist meeting—the World Bible Conference—was well attended in Philadelphia in 1919, Dr. William Bell Riley, a Minnesota minister, helped found the World Christian Fundamentals Association. By the early 1920s, fundamentalism had gained a major voice in American religion.

The Great Commoner

And within that collective voice, the outstanding individual voice belonged to none other than the Great Commoner himself, William Jennings Bryan, for over thirty years one of the leading politicians and far and away *the* leading religious speaker in the country. Interestingly, though a biblical literalist throughout his life, he had not always been an antievolutionist; as a young man, while he did not accept the theory of evolution, neither did he condemn it or its appearance in school curricula. As late as 1909, he had stated, "I am not yet convinced that man is a lineal descendant of the lower animals," but added, "I do not mean to find fault with you if you want to accept the theory."

Soon afterward, however, Bryan's attitude toward evolution changed profoundly. Among the factors that influenced this change was his exposure to the ideas in two controversial books. The first was *Belief in God and Immortality*, published in 1916 by James H. Leuba, an American psychology professor. In the book, Leuba reported the results of some informal polls he had taken suggesting that over half of the scientists in the United States doubted or denied the existence of God and that nearly half of graduating college students also expressed a lack of faith.

Bryan and the Cross of Gold

William Jennings Bryan, the influential politician and religious speaker whose presence at the Scopes trial helped to make that proceeding an international event, was born on March 19, 1860, in Salem, Illinois. After attending college, he practiced law in Illinois for a while, then moved to Lincoln, Nebraska, where he ran successfully for the U.S. Congress in 1890 and 1892. After leaving Congress, he briefly served as editor of the *Omaha World-Herald* and also began speaking at tent prayer meetings, an activity for which he became widely famous.

William Jennings Bryan

Bryan became even more famous as both orator and politician at the 1896 Democratic national convention, where he delivered his immortal "cross of gold" speech. The party was then divided between those who wanted the United States to remain on the gold standard and those who advocated the unlimited production of silver coins. A leading "free silverite," Bryan believed that the gold advocates represented a big-business conspiracy aimed at exploiting the "common people," of whom he saw himself as a champion. "You come to us and tell us that the great cities are in favor of the gold standard," he shouted from the podium at the gold advocates.

> We reply that the great cities rest upon our broad and fertile prairies. Burn down your cities and leave our farms, and your cities will spring up as if by magic; but destroy our farms and the grass will grow in the streets of every city in the country. . . . You shall not press down upon the brow of labor this crown of thorns. You shall not crucify mankind upon a cross of gold!

After a thunderous hour-long ovation and demonstration of support, Bryan received the nomination of his party and ran for president; but he lost the election to Republican candidate William McKinley. Nominated again in 1900 and still again in 1908, Bryan was defeated by Theodore Roosevelt and William H. Taft, respectively. Despite these setbacks, Bryan enjoyed the love and respect of millions of Americans and continued as a popular religious speaker. The cross and the crucifixion remained potent images and themes in his speeches.

This publication disturbed Bryan, who came to the conclusion that such loss of faith was directly proportional to the acceptance of evolutionist theory. In his speeches, he began to denounce evolution, saying that it "discredits things that are supernatural and encourages the worship of the intellect."

The other book that set Bryan firmly against evolution was Vernon Kellogg's 1917 exposé, *Headquarters Nights*. Kellogg, a biologist, suggested that the autocratic and militaristic German leaders, who were then attempting to conquer Europe in World War I, were proponents of a dangerous form of "Darwinism." Supposedly, they had applied the doctrine of the survival of the fittest to international relations by attempting to make Germany dominant over "inferior" nations. Horrified, Bryan now became convinced that the theory of evolution was an evil force that might tear apart societies, set nation against nation, and eventually result in humanity's ruin. "Survival of the fittest," he warned, might bring about "a life-and-death struggle from which sympathy and the spirit of brotherhood are eliminated. It is transforming the industrial world into a slaughter-house."

William Jennings Bryan blamed Darwin's theory of evolution for what he perceived as scientists' lack of faith in God.

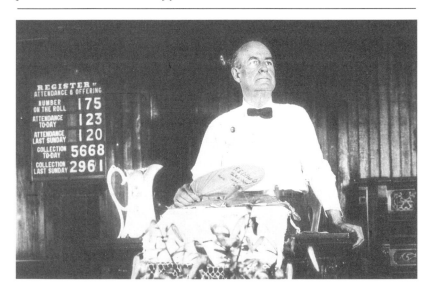

"No Adam, No Fall"

Thanks to Bryan and influential religious leaders who sympathized with his views, opposing the "dangerous" doctrine of evolution became a source of zeal and a defining cause of the fundamentalist movement. For both Bryan and increasing numbers of American fundamentalists, Darwin's theory seemed to cast doubt on the truth of long-cherished biblical characters and stories; therefore, it undermined basic religious tenets such as Adam and Eve's original sin and fall from grace, the necessity for prayer and penitence, and salvation. "No Adam, no fall," wrote one conservative preacher. "No fall, no atonement; no atonement, no Savior. Accepting evolution, how can we believe in a fall?" Bryan himself declared, "There is no place in evolution for the penitent soul; it knows no such transformation as being born again or having sins forgiven. [Evolution] robs a man's conscience of its compelling force."

By the early 1920s, all fundamentalists had come to agree that the most dangerous aspect of Darwin's theory was its "intrusion" into public school curricula, where it threatened to destroy the faith of a whole generation of children. "What shall it profit a man," Bryan thundered in his speeches, "if he shall gain all the learning of the schools and lose his faith in God?" This perceived threat against religious faith was the motivating factor behind the fundamentalist crusade to drive the teaching of evolution out of the schools.

The crusade's initial legal battles were unsuccessful. Among these were the attachment in 1921 of an antievolution clause to a financial bill in the South Carolina legislature; a 1922 Kentucky bill that would have banned the teaching of "Darwinism, atheism . . . and evolution insofar as it pertains to the origin of man"; in the same year another South Carolina bill, this one designed to withhold money from schools that taught "the cult known as Darwinism"; and similar antievolution bills in Florida and Texas.

Although for various reasons these particular bills never became law, the fundamentalists did manage to score some modest victories. In 1923, for example, Oklahoma passed a bill that banned textbooks containing descriptions of evolution (though the

The temptation of Eve and Adam and Eve's subsequent expulsion from the Garden of Eden. Fundamentalist Christians, who take such biblical stories as literal truth, opposed Darwin's theory of evolution and tried to ban the theory from being taught in the public schools.

actual teaching of evolution remained legal); and in North Carolina in 1924, despite the defeat of an antievolution bill in the state legislature, fearful school officials removed biology textbooks featuring chapters on evolution from all the state's high schools.

What seemed to be the fundamentalists' first *major* success came in 1925, when a Tennessee state legislator named John Washington Butler, a former farmer, introduced his own antievolution bill. As a devout Christian and biblical literalist, Butler's reasons for proposing the act were straightforward. "In the first place," he later wrote,

> the Bible is the foundation upon which our American government is built. . . . The evolutionist who denies the Biblical story of creation, as well as other Biblical accounts, cannot be a Christian. . . . It goes hand and hand with Modernism, makes Jesus Christ a faker, robs the Christian of his hope and undermines the foundation of our government.

The Butler Act, which prohibited the teaching of evolution and provided for penalties of from $100 to $500 (a substantial portion of an average teacher's salary at the time) for violators, passed the Tennessee legislature on March 13, 1925. The state's governor, Austin Peay, could have killed the bill by refusing to sign it. But he himself was a deeply religious man and perhaps saw in the rising tide of antievolution sentiment in the American South a social and political wave it would be expedient for him to ride. And so, on March 21 Peay signed the Butler Act into law, giving the following justification:

> After a careful examination I can find nothing of consequence in the books now being taught in our schools with which this bill will interfere in the slightest manner. Therefore it will not put our teachers in any jeopardy. Probably the law will never be applied. It may not be sufficiently definite to admit of any specific application or enforcement. Nobody believes that it is going to be an active statute.

TENNESSEE'S BUTLER ACT

This is the complete text of the controversial Butler Act, which the Tennessee legislature passed in March 1925:

An Act prohibiting the teaching of the Evolution Theory in all the Universities, Normals [state teachers colleges], and other public schools of Tennessee, which are supported in whole or in part by the public school funds of the State, and to provide penalties for the violations thereof.

Section 1. Be it enacted by the General Assembly of the State of Tennessee, That it shall be unlawful for any teacher in any of the Universities, Normals and other public schools of the State which are supported in whole or in part by the public school funds of the State, to teach any theory that denies the story of the Divine Creation of man taught in the Bible, and to teach instead that man has descended from a lower order of animals.

Section 2. Be it further enacted, That any teacher found guilty of the violation of this Act shall be guilty of a misdemeanor and upon conviction, shall be fined not less than One Hundred ($100.00) Dollars nor more than Five Hundred ($500.00) Dollars for each offense.

Section 3. Be it further enacted, That this Act take effect from and after its passage, the public welfare requiring it.

If Governor Peay's belief that the new law would "never be applied" was genuine and sincere, he was about to have the rudest awakening of his life. The forces of fundamentalism, led by Bryan, Butler, and others, were marching resolutely in one single-minded direction, while the forces of modern science, equally resolute, were rolling headlong in another. These forces would soon collide in a Tennessee courtroom, creating shock waves that continue to reverberate even today.

Chapter 2

Popcorn Merchants Vying with Evangelists: The Dayton Carnival

O N MAY 7, 1925, ABOUT SIX WEEKS after the passage of the Butler Act forbidding the teaching of evolution in Tennessee schools, Dayton high school teacher John Scopes was arrested for breaking the new law. Ironically, though rising fundamentalist ire over "godless" and "corrupting" evolutionist ideas had inspired the law, Scopes's arrest was not, as might be supposed, the result of a witch-hunt by local religious fanatics. Instead, the arrest and the trial that grew out of it were part of an orchestrated plot by prominent local citizens and officials, Scopes himself among them. Some of these men thought the Butler Act was unfair, unnecessary, and educationally backward, while others held that the law might be a good thing. Out of their spirited discussion of the matter emerged their primary goal—to test whether the new law was constitutional.

The Dayton "conspirators" also unanimously agreed that such a test case would attract attention to their tiny, out-of-the-way town and maybe help drum up some business. None of them at that moment foresaw that the case would garner international attention; that political and legal titans would descend on Dayton to do battle for the minds of future American generations; and that interest in and news coverage of this confrontation would for a while impart to their sleepy little village of 1,800 souls a loud and bizarre carnival-like atmosphere. In a way, as Scopes himself later put it, "It was just a drugstore discussion that got past control."

John Scopes Gives In

The immediate chain of events that led to Scopes's arrest began shortly after a Tennessee newspaper carried a small story about the new Butler Act. Most people in Tennessee did not see the story and most of those who did, with the exception of a few fundamentalists, showed little interest in it; but in faraway New York City, a secretary named Lucile Milner read the piece with great interest. Milner worked for the American Civil Liberties Union, or ACLU, and her job was to scan newspapers from around the country in search of stories that involved civil liberties, or citizens' constitutional rights. The ACLU had been established about six years before. Its main goals were (and still are) to uphold and defend the U.S. Constitution, especially the Bill of Rights, against unjust and unfair laws, and to provide free legal aid to people prosecuted under such laws, particularly poor and illiterate people who otherwise would be inadequately defended. Recognizing that the Butler Act was a potential violation of the freedoms of speech and religion, Milner passed the article along to her supervisors.

The ACLU eventually informed all Tennessee's newspapers that it would finance a legal test case of the new law if a local teacher who had broken it would willingly step forward and stand trial. On May 4, 1925, the Chattanooga *Daily Times*, one of Tennessee's largest papers, mentioned the ACLU's offer. That same day, George W. Rappelyea, a mining engineer who managed the Cumberland Coal and Iron Company in Dayton, read the *Times* article. Having studied geology and other sciences in college, Rappelyea strongly supported the theory of evolution and was dead set against the Butler Act; consequently, he found the idea of testing and perhaps nullifying the law appealing.

Rappelyea made some phone calls, and the next day the fateful meeting took place at the local drugstore, owned by Frank Robinson, who was also head of the county board of education. Besides Rappelyea and Robinson, the others in attendance were Walter White, the county superintendent of schools, and two local lawyers, Sue Hicks (a man who had been named after his mother) and Wallace C. Haggard. After a lengthy discussion, these men decided that having the test case in Dayton would be a good idea, partly as a way of drawing visitors to the town and thereby giving local businessmen a boost.

They then sent for John Scopes, the high school's twenty-four-year-old science teacher and football coach. Rappelyea pitched the idea of the test case to Scopes, who at first was very reluctant to get involved. On the one hand, the young man was modest, private, and nervous about being the focus of so much publicity; on the other, as a law-abiding citizen he understandably did not want to have an arrest record. But the other men kept pressing him. "It's a bad law," Rappelyea insisted. "Let's get rid of it. I will swear out a warrant and have you arrested. . . . That will make a big sensation. Why not bring a lot of doctors and preachers here? Let's get H. G. Wells [the world-renowned writer of popular fiction] and a lot of big fellows."

Years later, George Rappelyea holds a photo of Robinson's Drug Store, where he and others decided to come up with a test case to challenge the Butler Act. Rappelyea swore out a warrant against John Scopes for teaching evolution in the schools.

From left to right, George Rappelyea, Professor Walter White, Clay Green, and R. E. Robinson, were some of the men who instigated the trial of John Scopes.

Finally, John Scopes gave in. The excited Rappelyea immediately telegraphed the ACLU in New York announcing that a local teacher was willing to test the Butler Act; and the ACLU just as quickly responded with the message, "We will cooperate [in the] Scopes case with financial help, legal advice and publicity." Two days later, on May 7, Rappelyea, aided by Sue Hicks, wrote out the arrest warrant and Scopes himself hunted down a sheriff, who made the formal arrest. The following Saturday, the teacher stood before three local justices of the peace, holding the biology text he had used in his classes. He showed the magistrates passages from the book describing how some life-forms evolved into others, and, finding that the teaching of such material was a clear violation of the new law, they went through the motions of binding him over for trial. The legal wheels had begun to turn in what would become one the most famous and controversial trials of the twentieth century.

SCOPES INDICTED BY A SPECIAL GRAND JURY

According to the law, before John Scopes could be tried in court for violating the Butler Act, he had to be indicted, or formally accused, by a grand jury, a preliminary, pretrial jury consisting of several citizens sworn in by a judge. A grand jury's task is to decide whether the evidence collected by the prosecution warrants bringing the accused person to trial. On May 25, 1925, local judge John Raulston, worried that waiting for the regular grand jury to meet might cause Dayton to lose the trial to another town, convened a special grand jury, which promptly indicted Scopes. In his autobiography, published in 1932, Scopes's leading defense attorney, Clarence Darrow, recalled this unusual turn of events:

John T. Scopes

The judge called a special grand jury to indict John T. Scopes. This indicates how seriously that part of Tennessee viewed the heinous offense of teaching evolution, which they all pronounced as though the word began with double EE. The special grand jury was not legal, as the regular grand jury was to convene in a few weeks and the statute provided that a special grand jury could not be called excepting as a certain length of time intervened before the regular [trial] jury could assemble and be available. But even though the statute forbade the calling of the special grand jury, the crime was so terrible that the case could not be delayed. Then, too, there were other towns in the state that wanted the case, and the judge meant that Dayton should have the honor of prosecuting the boy for teaching science, and he himself would have the glory of defending The Faith. Of course, I do not know that this had anything to do with his calling the special grand jury. . . . Still, the treason against religion was reason enough for ignoring the law and resorting to a special session to bar the teaching of "EEvolution" in Tennessee.

A Giant in Their Midst

In the weeks that followed, the men who had originally con-cocted the idea for the trial began to realize that it was going to be a much more momentous event than they had anticipated. At first, they envisioned a prosecution team composed solely of local Tennessee lawyers. These eventually included Sue Hicks and his brother Herbert; Wallace Haggard; a former state assis-tant attorney general, Ben McKenzie and his son, J. Gordon McKenzie; and a county prosecutor named A. Thomas Stewart. All these men found themselves overshadowed, however, by a giant in their midst—the mighty orator William Jennings Bryan, who had volunteered to come to Dayton to help the prosecution.

People tended either to love Bryan or to hate him, for in his long public career he had championed many causes, all of which had been, in their times, controversial and divisive. Among these had been the right of women to vote; a government agency (the Department of Labor) to protect working people's rights; choos-ing senators by popular election (before 1913, state legislators

Citizens of Dayton meet with William Jennings Bryan in 1925 to discuss Bryan's involvement as a prosecutor in the Scopes trial. From left to right are Sue Hicks, J. G. McKenzie, Bryan, Herbert Hicks, Harry Lawrence, and Wallace Haggard.

chose them); and Prohibition, the law banning the sale and consumption of alcoholic beverages (which lasted from 1920 to 1933). But Bryan, whether one was for him or against him, was unquestionably a hugely important figure, and his pilgrimage to Dayton would surely thrust the town into the national limelight. He was also the chief spokesman for the American fundamentalist cause. Considering these credentials, the local attorneys were honored and only too happy to allow Bryan the starring role in the prosecution.

For Bryan himself, prosecuting and convicting Scopes seemed a way to make a greater public statement than any of the other political causes he had supported so far. As a sincere and devout fundamentalist, he had backed recent efforts to rid the schools of the "evil" influence of evolution; and here was what appeared to be a chance to prove science wrong and religion right on a national stage. In Pittsburgh, on May 13, he announced that he would act as spokesman for the World Christian Fundamentals Association at the Dayton trial, which was scheduled for July. "We cannot afford to have a system of education that destroys the religious faith of our children," he said in part. "There are about 5,000 scientists, and probably half of them are atheists, in the United States. Are we going to allow them to run our schools? We are not."

Darwin and Huxley His Companions

Hearing the news that Bryan would be involved in the case, several legal "heavyweights" offered to help defend Scopes and strike down the Butler Act. The prestigious defense team ended up including John R. Neal, former dean of the University of Tennessee's School of Law and one of the state's leading experts on the Constitution; Dudley Malone, a successful attorney who had been assistant secretary of state under President Woodrow Wilson in the late 1920s; and Arthur G. Hays, an ACLU lawyer and well-known expert on technical legal matters.

The prestigious reputations of these men notwithstanding, it soon became clear that the defense, like the prosecution, would be dominated by a single star. Clarence Darrow, the most renowned trial lawyer in the country, indeed probably in the

ATTORNEY FOR THE DAMNED

Clarence Darrow, John Scopes's chief counsel, and one of the most famous and skilled trial lawyers in American history, was born in Kinsman, Ohio, on April 18, 1857. After attending law school and passing the Ohio law bar, Darrow moved to Chicago, where he gained prominence as the general attorney for the Chicago and North Western Railway. He became a nationally known figure in 1895 when he defended Eugene V. Debs, president of the Railway Workers Union, who had been charged with violating court injunctions and inciting violence during a railroad strike.

Clarence Darrow

Although Darrow did not win the case, he managed to focus the country's attention on the plight of impoverished railroad workers, to halt attempts by railroad corporations to destroy the union, and to make himself a household name.

Thereafter, Darrow took on one controversial case after another, gaining a reputation as a man who hated injustice and human suffering and would gladly defend poor, downtrodden, and often hated and unpopular people. Dead set against capital punishment, he represented over fifty accused murderers, only one of whom ultimately suffered execution. Darrow also defended members of another unpopular and misunderstood group, conscientious objectors, young men who, for religious reasons, refused to serve in the army during World War I. In addition, he represented a "mad bomber" and communist revolutionaries.

In one of his most celebrated cases, Darrow defended two wealthy young men, Nathan Leopold and Richard Loeb, who had confessed to killing a fourteen-year-old boy "for the thrill of it." Darrow was responsible for obtaining life sentences instead of death for Leopold and Loeb. During this case, which riveted the nation, millions of people wondered why any decent person would help such disreputable characters; Darrow's response, as always, was that everyone, rich or poor, deserved the same opportunity for a legal defense. Darrow's attitude and choice of clients eventually inspired the title of his biography by Arthur Weinberg—*Attorney for the Damned*.

world, was drawn to Dayton because he personally detested the fundamentalists' agenda for censoring science in the schools and worried that their crusade might spread far and wide. "I had been a close observer of Mr. Bryan's campaigns against knowledge," Darrow later wrote, "and I was somewhat acquainted with history and felt that I knew what it meant. I knew how the bill [the Butler Act] . . . was put through, and they [fundamentalist leaders] had already announced that they would carry the campaign to every state in the Union."

Darrow was particularly critical of Bryan himself, saying that the Great Commoner knew too little about science to be interfering in science education. Instead, the blunt and witty Darrow pointed out, Bryan represented religion,

> and in this case he [Bryan] was the idol of all Morondom. His scientific aptitude was . . . stated in various speeches and interviews regarding what he did not know about science. He said that he was "not so much interested in the age of rocks as in the Rock of Ages [meaning traditional religion]." This left nothing more to be said by him to his credulous disciples who filled every hall and tent and crowded every grove when he appeared and defended The True Faith. . . . As to science, his mind was an utter blank.

By comparison, Darrow said of himself that he had grown up in a house where science was stressed and the books of Darwin, Huxley, and other famous scientists "had long been my companions." Not surprisingly, then, Darrow strongly believed that scientific truth would ultimately prevail over "the forces of ignorance." In response to Bryan's advance warning that the trial would be "a duel to the death," Darrow said, "We will smother Mr. Bryan's influence under a mountain of scientific testimony."

The Forces Against Satan

Like opposing armies massing for a great battle, the members of these legal teams began arriving in Dayton a few days before July 10, 1925, the day Scopes's trial was set to begin. The first

Clarence Darrow was critical of fundamentalist Christian beliefs that denied evolution as scientific fact.

team leader on the scene was Bryan. When his train pulled into the town's small station on the morning of July 7, a huge crowd of adoring fans greeted him as a conquering hero. Over the next two days, wearing a white pith helmet he had purchased in Panama and carrying a palm-leaf fan (the temperature soared to ninety in the shade), he walked the streets, chatting with locals and visitors alike.

On July 9, with less than twenty-four hours left before the trial's opening, Bryan made a speech to the sixteen members of the county board of education. Superintendent Walter White, one of the original drugstore conspirators, introduced him as "the greatest man in the world and its leading citizen." Bryan told those gathered that they should be proud of their stand against "godless" science, that the South's religious zeal was what set it apart from "less godly" sections of the country. He also revealed his true feelings about education, which, despite his listeners' admiration for him, must have made some of these educators uneasy. "To educate a man without giving him religion," Bryan declared, "is like sending out a ship without a pilot. If we have to give up either religion or education, we should give up education." After the speech, he and John Washington Butler, author of the law that had inspired the trial, placed their hands on a Bible and grinned widely as a photographer took their picture.

That night, Bryan's chief opponent arrived at the train station amidst far less fanfare than the Commoner had enjoyed. Clarence Darrow later recalled, "There was no torchlight parade to greet me as I stepped off the train. I did not miss it much, with the thermometer blazing away toward the hundred mark, where it remained nearly all the time we were there." Among the handful of well-wishers on the platform that night were Scopes and some of the Dayton residents who had arranged for Darrow's living accommodations. The tall northern lawyer was undoubtedly a bit surprised by the warmth of the hospitality he encountered. "As a matter of fact," he wrote,

> all through the event down there people treated us [Darrow and his wife Ruby, who arrived the day after he did] with extreme consideration in many ways, in spite of the fact that they must have been shocked by my position in the case. The banker of the town went off to the foothills . . . in order that we should have a cottage to ourselves in the village, which was so crowded that it became practically impossible to get accommodations of any sort.

Darrow did not exaggerate about the crowds that now thronged tiny Dayton's once quiet streets. People of every walk of life had come from all corners of Tennessee, from neighboring states, and from many other parts of the country to see Bryan in the flesh, or to witness history in the making, or to express their support for one side or the other. Among their number were many evangelists, zealous Christians seeking to preach and spread the teachings of the New Testament Gospels. Seeing the potential for profit, merchants and hawkers of every description also descended on the town, transforming it into what some people now laughingly (and others *not* so laughingly) called "the Dayton carnival." Darrow perfectly captured the colorful, festive, and often strange atmosphere in this excerpt from his autobiography:

> "Hot dog" booths and fruit peddlers and ice cream vendors and sandwich sellers had sprung into existence like

mushrooms on every corner and everywhere between, mingling with the rest, ready to feed the throng. Evangelist tents were propped up at vantage points around the town square. . . . They [the preachers] were crying out against the wickedness of Darwin and the rest of us, and advocating as substitutes cool meadows and melodious harps in KINGDOM COME. . . . Popcorn merchants and sleight-of-hand artists vied with evangelists for the favor and custom of the swarms that surged back and forth along the few squares that were the center of the community; speeches were bawled at street corners under the glare of trying artificial-lighting arrangements; the vendors raised their voices to drown the evangelists who were the old-time sort who seemed to believe every word they said and were really interested in saving souls; and each worked his own side of the street, up and down. Then over the river, under the trees, a band of Holy Rollers [Christian fundamentalists who express their religious fervor in physical displays] gathered every night. As they grew excited and shouted and sang and twitched and twirled, the people crowded closer around them in curiosity and wonder. . . . All sorts of weird cults were present in Dayton, all joining forces to put up a strong fight against Satan and his cohorts.

A Packed Courthouse

On Friday morning, July 10, 1925, Darrow, wearing suspenders over a tan shirt, wound his way through the obstacle course of popcorn vendors and Bible sellers to the courthouse. Along the way he passed numerous huge signs bearing messages such as "Come to Jesus," "Prepare to meet thy Maker," and "Read your Bible daily," which gave a clear indication of the sentiments of his opposition. The lawn in front of the courthouse was jammed with people, as were the building's corridors, so it took the chief defender several minutes to reach the courtroom on the second floor.

On entering the courtroom, Darrow saw that all its four hundred

Anti-evolution books are sold in Dayton at the opening of the Scopes trial.
For the most part, the citizens of Dayton supported William Jennings Bryan.

seats were taken and at least another three hundred spectators
stood in whatever spaces they could find. More than a hundred
reporters packed the press tables, while John Scopes sat at the
defense table and the judge, John Raulston, a Dayton resident,
was already perched behind the judge's bench. Prosecutors Ben
and J. Gordon McKenzie were there, too, and Darrow greeted
them amiably. "Well," Darrow said to Ben McKenzie, "I see
you, too, wear suspenders." "Yes, Colonel Darrow," McKenzie
replied, "we have to keep our pants up down here in Tennessee
just like you do up there in Chicago." Darrow was amused that
local officials had conferred on him the honorary title of
"Colonel," which put him on an even footing with the other
prominent southern gentlemen present, who routinely
addressed one another as "General," "Colonel," and "Captain."

Judge John F. Raulston, trial judge in the Scopes trial.

A few minutes later, Darrow and the others heard the large crowd burst into an enthusiastic round of applause. The Great Commoner had made his grand entrance. As he made his way to the prosecution table, Bryan smiled broadly and nodded his head, acknowledging the display of adulation. When the demonstration finally died down, Judge Raulston asked a local clergyman to open the proceeding with a prayer, a custom not widespread in Tennessee courtrooms but one Raulston often observed. Bryan and most others automatically bowed their heads, but Darrow, his expression betraying his surprise, just kept looking around the room. "This was new to me," he later wrote. "I had practiced law for more than forty years, and had never before heard God called in to referee a court trial."

Considering the religious overtones of the case, Darrow thought the prayer was inappropriate and gave an unfair advantage to the prosecution. Immediately, he knew that one of his first tasks in John Scopes's defense must be to move that the judge eliminate the daily opening prayer. Darrow realized that raising such an objection in the shadow of a banner bearing the admonishment "Read your Bible daily" was not going to increase his popularity with the thousands of devoted Bible readers gathered in Dayton. But he had traveled there to defend academic freedom, not to win a popularity contest. His legal opposition would soon learn that his reputation as a brilliant, relentlessly hard-fighting, and boldly direct trial attorney was extremely well deserved.

Chapter 3

Marching Backward to the Middle Ages: The Defense's Opening Volley

Darrow decided to postpone his planned objection to the practice of having a minister begin each court session with a prayer until the actual trial had gotten under way. The initial session on July 10, 1925, was devoted mainly to picking a jury, a process Darrow had assumed would take at least a few days. Each prospective juror had to be interviewed by both the prosecution and the defense, and Scopes's attorneys were prepared to argue long and hard over finding the right people to weigh the controversial evidence.

As it turned out, however, selecting the jury proved to be a fairly short and painless process. Darrow did politely excuse a few of those he interviewed, including Tom Jackson, a former serviceman who claimed he had formed his opinion about evolution from reading the Bible. When Reverend J. P. Massingill took the stand, Darrow asked him if he had ever preached for or against evolution. After first trying to evade the question, Massingill suddenly and proudly declared, "Well, I preached against it, of course!" to which the audience responded with applause and "Amens." "Why 'of course'?" Darrow inquired, but already knowing the answer he avoided an argument and simply dismissed the clergyman.

As the morning wore on, the prosecution and defense accepted most of the prospective jurors. Typical was the friendly exchange Darrow had with a local farmer named Jim Riley. The attorney asked if Riley had ever discussed the subject of evolution with anyone and Riley answered that he had not. "Ever hear Mr. Bryan speak about it?" Darrow inquired.

"No, sir," Riley answered in a southern drawl.

"Ever read anything he said about it?"

"No, sir." And then Riley admitted, "I can't read."

"Well, you are fortunate," said Darrow with a sympathetic grin and promptly accepted the man onto the jury.

To Darrow's surprise, by the end of the opening session, the Scopes trial had its jury; but he, like his legal colleagues, realized that the preliminaries were not yet over. In the trial's second session, scheduled for Monday, July 13, before addressing Scopes's actual guilt or innocence the opposing attorneys would debate whether the Butler Act itself was constitutional.

The jury selected to try the Scopes case. Jury selection moved quickly, with few potential jurors eliminated.

A Violation of State and Federal Civil Rights?

The weather that Monday morning was as hot, sticky, and uncomfortable as it had been in the preceding week. Judge Raulston benefited from an electric fan set up near his bench, while the attorneys, jurors, and spectators had to content themselves with handheld fans. After everyone was assembled, Raulston delayed opening the session long enough for some radio engineers to adjust their equipment. This was the first court trial ever to be broadcast live over the radio, a fact that greatly pleased Raulston, who was planning to run for reelection in the near future. "My gavel will be heard around the world," he boasted.

After the opening prayer, prosecutor Stewart stood and read the indictment, the formal accusation against Scopes. No one present, including Scopes and his lawyers, in any way disputed that the teacher had broken the law as it was laid down in Butler's statute. The question at hand was whether the law itself was valid under the Tennessee constitution and the U.S. Constitution; and Scopes's defense team now attempted to discredit the Butler Act in order to quash, or throw out, the indictment. If the team accomplished this goal, the only way the prosecution would be able to keep the law on the books would be to appeal the case to the state's supreme court.

John Neal was the first defense counsel to move that the indictment be quashed, claiming that the Butler Act violated Tennessee's constitution on thirteen counts. In particular, he argued, Article 11, section 12, required that "knowledge, learning and virtue being essential to the preservation of republican institutions, and the diffusion of the opportunities and advantages of education . . . it shall be the duty of the general assembly [the state legislature] . . . to cherish literature and science." Neal insisted that by teaching evolution, a principle recognized by scientists everywhere, John Scopes was merely following the state's constitutional directive to "cherish science." Said Neal, the Butler Act also violated state laws that protected all citizens' rights "to worship Almighty God according to the dictates of their own conscience," to freedom of speech, and to due process of law.

THE ARGUMENTS OVER THE FOURTEENTH AMENDMENT

In their opening motions to quash the indictment against their client, Scopes's attorneys claimed that the Butler Act violated Section 1 of the Fourteenth Amendment to the U.S. Constitution. This statute states, in part:

> No state shall make or enforce any law which shall abridge the privileges or immunities of citizens of the United States; nor shall any state deprive any person of life, liberty, or property, without due process of law; nor deny to any person within its jurisdiction the equal protection of the laws.

Seen in conference at the defense table are Dudley Malone and Arthur G. Hays (back row), and Thomas Scopes and John Scopes (seated).

Scopes's defenders focused primarily on the phrases "due process of law" and "equal protection of the laws," pointing out that both forbid any state from denying a citizen most of the rights granted under the Bill of Rights. Among these rights are freedom of speech and of religion. According to the defense, by indicting Scopes for teaching evolution, which the teacher personally believed to be the explanation for the creation of life, the state of Tennessee had denied him his right to believe whatever he wanted and to speak openly about that belief. In rejecting this argument, Judge Raulston echoed the prosecution's claim that Scopes's rights had not been violated because the state had not interfered in his private life. Scopes had been *hired* and was *paid* to teach whatever the state and the public school system deemed appropriate; if he thought the material inappropriate, he had every right to apply for a job in a private school.

The defense attorneys offered other arguments against the Butler Act. In addition to violating the state's constitution, they contended, it contradicted Section 1 of the Fourteenth Amendment to the U.S. Constitution, which forbids infringement of life, liberty, or property without due process of law. Arthur Hays rose and made a motion to quash on the basis that the antievolution law "unreasonably extended the police powers of the state" and thereby infringed on Scopes's rights as an individual. And Dudley Malone made the telling point that the Butler Act imposed on all Tennesseans a specific religious opinion taken from a particular religious book to which only some people ascribed.

(Above) Dr. John Neal and (right) Arthur G. Hays tried to have the Butler Act overturned before the commencement of the trial.

At the conclusion of the defense's constitutional arguments, it was the prosecution's turn to rebut them. Before doing so, Stewart asked Judge Raulston to remove the jurors, who had not yet been sworn in: Since their duty was to judge the actual evidence of Scopes's crime and that evidence was yet to be presented, their presence during these legal arguments was optional. Stewart claimed he would feel "more at ease" with the jury "out," although his real motive was likely a fear that the ongoing arguments might sway the jurors against the Butler Act. Overruling Darrow's objection, Raulston complied, and a court officer led the jurors out onto the courthouse lawn. There, ironically, they could still hear the proceedings over loudspeakers that had been set up for the crowds who were unable to squeeze into the courtroom.

A Book of Morals, Not Science

After the prosecutors strenuously argued that the defense's motions to quash were just so much hot air and that the antievolution law was perfectly legal, the judge adjourned for lunch. When court reconvened in the afternoon, Darrow stood up to

Dudley Malone outlines the case from the defense's viewpoint during the Scopes trial.

make his first real speech of the trial. These words were intended as a general summary of the defense's viewpoint in the case. According to a *New York Times* reporter, at that moment all the people in the huge crowd craned their necks to get a good look at "the bent figure with the seamed [wrinkled] brown face and the great head. He was in his shirt sleeves, his purple suspenders standing out against his shirt."

Darrow began by calling the Butler Act "as brazen and bold an attempt to destroy learning as was ever made in the Middle Ages." Then he turned to William Jennings Bryan, who had so far remained quiet. As was his way, Darrow did not mince words; he stated in no uncertain terms that Bryan was more responsible than anyone else for this "foolish, mischievous and wicked act." Gasps rippled through the audience as Bryan's many fans bristled at hearing him so insulted, while the Commoner himself, biding his time for his own chance to speak, maintained his composure and his silence. "The state of Tennessee," Darrow continued,

> under an honest and fair interpretation of the constitution, has no more right to teach the Bible as the divine book than that the Koran [the Muslim holy book] is one, or the book of Mormons or the book of Confucius [the Chinese philosopher] or the Buddha [the Indian holy man] or the Essays of [poet Ralph Waldo] Emerson or any one of the ten thousand books to which human souls have gone for consolation and aid in their troubles.

Darrow paced slowly, sometimes speaking quietly while dropping his head and hunching his shoulders, as if brooding. Then he would suddenly straighten up, shoot his head forward, and loudly make a point in a veritable torrent of indignant words and phrases. He said that he understood how the Bible consoled and comforted many people and that he had no "fault to find" with anyone who felt that way about the Bible or any other book. "But the Bible is not one book," he pointed out. "The Bible is made up of sixty-six books written over a period of about one thousand years. . . . It is a book primarily of religion and morals. It is not a book of science. Never was and was never meant to be."

Lawyer Clarence Darrow was well known for his mesmerizing presence.

Following this line of reasoning, Darrow argued that by making it a criminal offense to teach any but the biblical account of creation, the state was setting the Bible up as "the yardstick to measure every man's intelligence . . . and learning." In that case, he suggested in a bold, flippant tone, if a person was deficient in math, philosophy, or chemistry, he or she would have nowhere else to go but the Bible for the answers; and every scrap of human knowledge would be submitted to a religious test.

An Audacious Performance

The longer Darrow railed on, the more his performance gripped and mesmerized the spectators. Some of them were clearly impressed by his commanding presence and the great force of his arguments, while many others, horrified by what they considered a shameful attack on God and the Bible, sat in stunned silence. But what they had heard thus far had been merely a preamble to his most important point, which he now delivered in an intense, passionate, and devastating display of logic and courtroom theatrics. "If today you can take a thing like evolution and make it a crime to teach it in the public schools," he warned,

> tomorrow you can make it a crime to teach it in the private schools. And the next year you can make it a crime to teach it in the church. And the next session you may ban books and the newspapers. Soon you may set Catholic against Protestant and Protestant against

Protestant and try to foist your own religion upon the mind of man. If you can do one you can do the other. Ignorance and fanaticism are ever busy and need feeding. Always they are feeding and gloating for more. After a while, your honor, it is setting man against man and creed against creed until with flying banners and beating drums we are marching backward to the glorious ages of the sixteenth century when bigots lighted fagots [bundles of twigs] to burn the man who dared to bring any intelligence and enlightenment and culture to the human mind.

His powerful speech over, Darrow sighed and shrugged. At that moment, one of the watching journalists wrote, "In one of his great leisurely shrugs, in which his whole torso participates, he can put more contempt, more combativeness, more of a sense of reserve power, than anyone else can express in a dozen gestures." After Darrow's audacious and effective performance, none of the prosecutors were anxious to try to top it; Judge Raulston seemed also to sense the air of emotional climax and finality the chief defense counsel had created and deemed it prudent to adjourn for the day.

In the late afternoon, as Darrow and his wife walked back toward their lodgings, prosecutor Ben McKenzie came up and threw an arm around the older man's shoulder. "It was the greatest speech I have ever heard in my life on any subject," McKenzie admitted. These words undoubtedly echoed the feelings of many who had been in the courtroom that day.

Darrow's Thunderbolt

Having made such a bold and controversial opening impression, in which he had publicly stated his reservations about the dangers of fundamentalist intolerance, Darrow decided that he might as well go ahead and tackle the touchy subject of the daily prayer. In private, he and some of his colleagues told the judge that they "did not consider it fair or suitable to play up [the prosecution's] side by opening court proceedings with prayer; it was

Clarence Darrow and Ben McKenzie
confer during the Scopes trial.

not a form of church service; it was a trial in a court; and at best it was an unfair weapon to introduce, particularly as the case had a religious aspect."

Judge Raulston, who believed there could be no harm in prayer under any circumstances, appeared to be unmoved by this argument. So when the third session convened on Tuesday morning, July 14 (with the jurors still relegated to the front lawn), Darrow immediately protested in open court. "I don't object to the jury or anyone else praying in secret or in private," he said. "But I do object to the turning of this courtroom into a [religious] meetinghouse in the trial of this case. This case is a conflict between science and religion, and no attempt should be made by means of prayer to influence the deliberation and consideration by the jury of the facts in this case."

At these words, a sudden hush fell over the hall. "The people assembled looked as though a thunderbolt had stunned them," Darrow later recalled, "and the wrath of the Almighty might be hurled down upon the heads of the defense." None of the members of this mainly devoutly religious audience had ever heard of any sort of objection to saying a prayer and they were shocked to say the least. Raulston, a little hurt, more than a little angry, and still completely unmoved by the defense's argument, denied the request to strike the daily prayer.

The judge refused to budge on the defense's constitutional arguments as well. The next day, Wednesday, July 15, he

AGNOSTIC OR INFIDEL?

On Tuesday, July 14, 1925, after his unsuccessful objection to the judge's ordering of a prayer to open the proceedings each morning, defense attorney Clarence Darrow raised another objection. Earlier, prosecutor A. Thomas Stewart had publicly, and in an unflattering tone, labeled Darrow an "agnostic" and an "infidel." An agnostic is one who sees no evidence for God's existence, yet does not deny that a supreme deity might exist, and therefore has an open mind about religion (as opposed to an atheist, who states categorically that there is no God). By contrast, the term "infidel" is usually used in a derogatory way by persons of one religion to describe someone who does not share their views.

Attorney A. Thomas Stewart accuses Darrow of being an "infidel."

Darrow had no qualms about Stewart calling him an agnostic, for it was no secret that Darrow *was* one. In fact, his own client, Scopes, had earlier stated, "Yes, I consider Mr. Darrow an agnostic, but as such that would not prejudice any fair-minded juror. I call myself an agnostic, but I am devoutly religious in my own way." Addressing the court, Darrow expressed the same sentiment, saying, "I do not consider it an insult, but rather a compliment, to be called an agnostic. I do not pretend to know, where many ignorant men are sure."

On the other hand, Darrow was thoroughly outraged that a Tennessee public official would call him an infidel, which he considered to be an inaccurate and unwarranted personal attack. For fifteen minutes, Darrow emotionally explained to the court that many people living in other lands looked on the "good Christians" sitting before him as infidels. It all depended on one's point of view. It was clear that the fundamentalists in the audience neither understood nor accepted this argument; but Judge Raulston, in a spirit of fairness, admonished Stewart, who reluctantly but politely apologized to Darrow.

The Rhea County courthouse in Dayton, the site of the Scopes trial. To the delight of many skeptical Daytonians, the clock always ran ten minutes late.

announced his refusal to quash the indictment. In a six-thousand-word ruling, a speech lasting about an hour, Raulston went through each of the defense motions one by one, explaining how, in his view, each was invalid or had no bearing on the case. Soon after he had finished, he called an early lunch break.

At one o'clock that afternoon, at long last the judge readmitted the jurors and swore them in. The part of the trial dealing directly with Scopes's "crime" of teaching evolution, which so many people had come from far and wide to see, could now begin. Many had also come to hear Bryan speak, to watch him unleash a verbal avalanche of fire and brimstone on Scopes, Darrow, and all others who dared to challenge God's "revealed word." And shortly after the jury-swearing, Bryan finally, although only very briefly, broke the silence he had so far maintained in the proceeding. When the prosecution objected to defense attorney Dudley Malone's reading from an essay Bryan had long ago written about religious freedom, the Commoner rose and stated he did not mind being quoted in the matter. Further, he did not need his colleagues' protection. He would make very clear where he stood on the topics at hand "when the proper time comes." Most of the onlookers applauded, sensing that their champion had already prepared a speech that he believed would both dazzle and damn the opposition. And they were right.

Chapter 4

Divine Plan or Ancestor in the Jungle? The Prosecution's Rigid Stance

ON WEDNESDAY AFTERNOON, JULY 15, 1925, with the technical arguments out of the way and the jury back in place, it was time for witnesses to be called for and against the defendant, John Scopes. The prosecution and defense each had a different strategy in questioning these witnesses. The prosecutors wanted mainly and simply to demonstrate that Scopes had broken the law by teaching evolution, whereas the defense was eager to present a broader interpretation of the "crime." According to defense attorney Dudley Malone, the exact wording of the Butler Act suggested that the defendant had been charged with two separate and distinct crimes. The first was teaching a theory that contradicted the biblical version of creation; the second was teaching that humans had evolved from lower forms of life. The defense seemed willing to concede that Scopes had taught about the mechanics of evolution. But it was prepared to show that the teacher had not presented to his students any information that directly contradicted the biblical account of creation. Malone stated, "We shall show that there are millions of people who believe in evolution *and* in the stories of creation as set forth in the Bible, and who find no conflict between the two."

53

With this statement, Malone had set forth the defense's strategy, which was in "the narrow purpose" to prove Scopes's innocence, and in "the broad purpose . . . to prove the Bible is a work of religious aspirations and rules of conduct which must be kept in the field of theology. . . . We maintain that science and religion embrace two separate and distinct fields of thought and learning." The meaning of this statement was clear to all. The defense intended to challenge attempts by fundamentalists to have their religious views replace science in school curricula.

It was also clear to those present that the prosecutor most capable of meeting the defense's challenge was William Jennings Bryan, who had come to Dayton eager to defend the fundamentalist position. There seemed to be little doubt among many of the devout spectators and listeners that the Commoner would soon deliver a speech that would counter and thoroughly demolish Darrow's opening "tirade."

The Witnesses Interrogated

Following the usual court procedure, the prosecution took the lead in calling witnesses. First on the stand was Walter White, the school superintendent and one of those who had originally convinced Scopes to test the law. White testified to prosecutor Stewart that during the meeting at Robinson's drugstore held in early May, Scopes had admitted to teaching his students about evolution.

A few minutes later, under cross-examination, White admitted to Darrow that the book Scopes had taught from, *Civic Biology*, had been used in the school system for many years and had been officially adopted by the state's textbook commission in 1919, six years before the trial. White also admitted that after the passage of the Butler Act in March 1925, he, as superintendent, had not warned Scopes or any other teacher against telling the students about evolution. Darrow was clearly trying to show that in teaching evolution Scopes was simply performing his job in the usual way and that Scopes's superiors originally had not taken the antievolution law seriously.

Next, the prosecution called two of Scopes's students, fourteen-year-old Howard Morgan (son of the banker who had loaned his

School superintendent Walter White testifies during the Scopes trial. White was one of the men who convinced Scopes to test the Butler Act.

house to the Darrows) and seventeen-year-old Harry Shelton. Both boys confirmed that the teacher had presented information in class about various kinds of life evolving from lower forms. According to Morgan, Scopes had taught that

> the earth was once a hot, molten mass, too hot for plant and animal life to exist upon it; in the sea the earth cooled off; there was a little germ of one-celled organism formed, and this organism kept evolving until it got to be a pretty good-sized animal and then came on to be a land animal, and it kept on evolving, and from this was man, and that man was just another mammal.

When Stewart asked Morgan if Scopes had defined the term "mammal" in class, several people in the audience led their small children out of the room and one woman put her fingers in her ears. Apparently these persons considered it indecent to

Students testify that John Scopes taught them about the theory of evolution, including the descent of humankind.

speak aloud about mammals bearing live young and suckling their offspring.

On cross-examining Morgan, Darrow asked, "He [Scopes] didn't say a cat was the same as a man?"

"No sir," the boy responded. "He said a man had a reasoning power; that these animals did not."

"There is some doubt about that," quipped Darrow, smiling. "But that is what he said, is it?"

A few minutes later, Darrow asked Harry Shelton if he had belonged to his local church both before and after hearing his teacher talk about evolution, and the young man confirmed that he had. "You didn't leave church when he told you all forms of life began with a single cell?" Darrow inquired. Shelton replied by repeating that he still attended church.

After calling the drugstore owner Frank Robinson to the stand to testify that he had heard Scopes admit to teaching about evolution, the prosecution rested its case. Apparently, Stewart

and his colleagues were satisfied that they had presented suffi-
cient evidence to show that the teacher had violated the Butler
Act. It was now the defense's turn to present its witnesses.

The defense called Dr. Maynard Metcalf, a zoologist for-
merly of Oberlin College and now associated with Johns Hop-
kins University. Because Metcalf was also a devout member of
the Congregational Church, Scopes's attorneys hoped to use him
as an example of someone who had accepted the scientific
explanation of creation without losing faith in God. "Do you
know any scientific man who is not an evolutionist?" Darrow
asked the witness.

Metcalf answered, "I am acquainted with practically all of
the zoologists, botanists, and geologists of this country—I know
there is not a single one among them that doubts the fact of evolution." The witness then went on to explain the theory that life
had begun in the sea; that life was at least 600 million years old;
that he could, if necessary, cite at least fifty ways that mammals
differed from other life-forms; and that human beings had
descended from early versions of primates, the zoological group
that includes apes, monkeys, baboons, and lemurs.

*The schoolhouse in Dayton, Tennessee, where John Scopes taught the theory of
evolution and other scientific principles and theories.*

OBSERVATIONS, FACTS, AND THEORIES

During his testimony, zoologist Maynard Metcalf, the defense's only expert witness to make it to the stand, explained what scientists meant by the term "theory" as in "theory of evolution." It meant a "logical explanation" for a set of known facts, he said, not a "guess," as most nonscientists assumed. Discussing definitions for the term "theory" for the *Encyclopaedia Britannica*, English philosophy professor Leonard J. Russell stated that a scientific theory "may be restricted to hypotheses that have been so strongly confirmed as to become part of the accepted doctrine of a particular science. In its best use, it signifies a systematic account of some field of study, derived from a general set of propositions." Thus, scientists first make observations and collect evidence and then go on to construct a theory that seems to explain all or most of the evidence; and such a theory can be tested and is subject to change based on new data.

Yet even when a theory like Darwin's changes, the basic facts that inspired it in the first place do not. As scientists Robert M. Hazen and James Trefil explain in their book *Science Matters*:

> One must distinguish between the *fact* of evolution and any particular *theory* of evolution, a distinction that will become clear if you think about [theories of] gravity, from Newton to Einstein. . . . Any one of these theories may be wrong, incomplete, or incorporated into another. But if you drop an object, it falls, regardless of which theory you believe. That is the fact of gravity. In the same way, the fossil record, molecular biology, and geological research all buttress the notion that modern complex life on earth evolved out of earlier, simpler forms. This is the fact of evolution. As with gravity, there are many theories of evolution that purport to describe this process. Any one of them, starting with Darwin's, may be wrong or incomplete. The correctness or incorrectness of any particular theory, however, doesn't change the fact of evolution, any more than one can question the fact of gravity.

Bryan Speaks at Last

When the judge adjourned court late on Wednesday afternoon, Metcalf had not completed his testimony. So when the trial reconvened on Thursday morning, Darrow attempted to put the scientist back on the stand for some final questions. But the prosecution vigorously objected. Stewart contended that all testimony bearing on the meaning of evolution or its truth or falsity had nothing to do with whether John Scopes had broken the law and should therefore be excluded from the trial. Darrow responded that reaching a clearer understanding about evolution *was* relevant to the case and said that the defense planned to put other expert witnesses besides Metcalf on the stand.

Thus, the trial had reached another procedural impasse. It could not proceed until the judge had made a ruling on whether to allow the defense to present its expert witnesses. Once more, Judge Raulston dismissed the jury from the courtroom, while the prosecution and defense prepared to argue the matter. For the remainder of the morning, various members of the prosecution team told the court why they thought no other scientists should be allowed to testify. Finally, at about 11:45 A.M., the judge adjourned for lunch.

A few minutes after court reconvened in the afternoon, a sudden hush fell over the crowd and all eyes in the packed courtroom riveted on the stout, balding man who now stood beside the prosecution table. William Jennings Bryan was about to deliver the state's final argument for disallowing the defense's expert witnesses. For his many fans, as Tom McGowen puts it,

> this was the moment they had been waiting for. Now their great crusading leader would use his marvelous powers of oratory to flatten and bewilder Darrow and the other "atheistic" defense attorneys, to show that evolution was nothing but groundless nonsense, and to prove that the words of the Bible were the underlying truth. They felt that the trial would soon be over.

"My friends," Bryan's big voice boomed. And then he suddenly paused and addressed the judge. "I beg your pardon, if the court please, I have been so in the habit of talking to an audience instead of a court that I will sometimes say 'my friends,' although I happen to know that not all of them are my friends." The audience laughed heartily at this pointed jab at Scopes and his defense team. Then, sensing that the crowd was with him, Bryan began delivering his prepared remarks.

William Jennings Bryan delivers his arguments for disallowing the defense's expert witnesses.

The people of this state knew what they were doing when they passed the [Butler] law, and they knew the dangers of the [evolutionist] doctrine, knew that they did not want it taught to their children. It isn't proper to bring experts in here to try to defeat the purpose of the people of this state by trying to show that what they denounce and outlaw is a beautiful thing that everybody ought to believe in.

Applause rang through the courtroom as the audience signaled its approval of this opening statement.

As Bryan continued, more applause, as well as rounds of laughter, periodically punctuated his speech. He vehemently attacked Dr. Metcalf's testimony; but since Bryan lacked the knowledge needed for a true scientific rebuttal, he skillfully avoided the actual issue of evolution and resorted mostly to numerous little asides and jokes about the animal kingdom. Some were clearly inane—for instance, his remark that he would try to estimate the number of the world's animal species in round numbers even though animals did not reproduce in round numbers. Yet such quips were designed to please the crowd and sure enough, they elicited the expected supportive laughter and applause. In their own ignorance of the workings of evolution, many of the spectators actually believed that Bryan was disproving Metcalf, and Darwin along with him.

"Amens" in the Record

After concluding his attack on evolution by claiming it to be nothing more than conjecture and guesswork unsupported by facts, Bryan launched into a special version of one of his patented tent-meeting sermons. "The Bible is the word of God," he affirmed jubilantly.

A British cartoon mocks evolution by picturing Darwin as half monkey attempting to show his close relative the resemblance between them.

The Bible is the only expression of man's hope of salvation. The Bible, the record of the Son of God, the Savior of the world, born of the Virgin Mary, crucified and risen again. That Bible is not going to be driven out of this court by experts who have come hundreds of miles to testify that they can reconcile evolution with its ancestor in the jungle, with man made by God in His image, man put here for purposes as a part of the divine plan.

Loud "Amens," exactly like those in a revival meeting, sounded from the back of the room. More than a little irritated, Darrow told the judge, "I want those 'Amens' to be put in the record."

Bryan seemed pleased by the crowd's response and also by the fact that it had annoyed Darrow. Encouraged, the Commoner raised his great voice to the rafters and delivered a mighty finale to his oration. The principle of evolution was dangerous, he said, because it disputed the occurrence of miracles.

> There is no place for the miracles in this train of evolution, and the Old Testament and the New are filled with miracles. If this doctrine is true . . . [it] eliminates every mystery in the . . . [Bible] and eliminates everything supernatural, and that means they eliminate the virgin birth—that means they eliminate the resurrection of the body—that means they eliminate the doctrine of atonement and that they believe man has been rising all the time, that man never fell, that when the Savior came there was not any reason for his coming. . . . When the Christians of this state have tied their hands and said, "We will not take advantage of our power to teach religion to children by teachers paid by us," these people [Darrow and the other famous defense attorneys] come in from the outside . . . and force upon the people of this state a doctrine that refuses not only their belief in God but their belief in a Savior and belief in heaven and takes from them every moral standard that the Bible gives us!

No more than a second after the conclusion of the speech, the crowd erupted into a thunderous and tumultuous ovation. Dozens of people, some with tears streaming down their cheeks, leapt from their seats and crowded around Bryan, congratulating him and patting him on the back. As he soaked up this adulation, the obviously befuddled and exasperated Darrow asked Arthur Hays, "Can it be possible that this trial is taking place in the twentieth century?"

As it turned out, Darrow had even more to be upset about. That same day, responding to Bryan's arguments, Dudley Malone delivered a reasoned and spirited speech justifying the defense's calling of expert witnesses; but the next morning, Friday, July 17,

"WE ARE NOT AFRAID"

After William Jennings Bryan's boisterous and well-received speech, in which he rejected the defense's desire to call expert witnesses and defended the position that the entire Bible is literally true, defense attorney Dudley Malone responded with a rousing speech of his own. "We have been told that this was not a religious question," said Malone. "I defy anybody, after Mr. Bryan's speech, to believe that this was not a religious question." Malone then accused the prosecution of trying to destroy science in order to maintain belief in the Bible. He called for giving "the next generation all the facts, all the available data, all the information that learning, that study, that observation had produced." Instead of forcing students to choose between scientific and theological ideas about the world, why not let them have both?

John Scopes (left) with Dudley Malone during the trial of the century.

Fighting for the defense's right to present its expert witnesses, Malone shouted that such experts "have a right to testify in support of our view that the Bible is not to be taken literally as an authority in a court of law." Resolutely, he asked, "Are we to hold mankind to a literal understanding of the claim that the world is six thousand years old because of the limited vision of men [the Bible's ancient authors] who believed the world was flat and that the earth was the center of the universe? Are we to have our children know nothing about science except what the church says they shall know?" Staring directly at Bryan, Malone declared, "We feel we stand with progress. We feel we stand with science. We feel we stand with intelligence. We feel we stand with fundamental freedom in America. We are not afraid."

In conclusion, Malone asked Judge Raulston to allow the defense witnesses to testify "as a matter of justice for the defense in this case!" The speech was so eloquent and passionate that the audience, even including many of the fundamentalists who supported Bryan, gave Malone a long and respectful ovation. However, none of this had any discernible effect on the judge, who ended up disallowing the expert witnesses.

William Jennings Bryan poses with admirers in Dayton, Tennessee.

Judge Raulston ruled in favor of the prosecution. The trial had to do only with John Scopes's breaking of a state law, he said. Since science and religion "were not the issue," the defense's request for more expert witnesses was hereby denied.

Because the defense had no other witnesses to call, it now appeared to nearly everyone that the trial was basically over. However, the stubborn and always calculating Clarence Darrow had not yet admitted defeat. He still had one last ace up his sleeve and when court reconvened on the following Monday, he would play it.

Chapter 5

A Clash of Giants: Clarence Darrow Versus William Jennings Bryan

W HEN THE SCOPES TRIAL RECONVENED on Monday, July 20, 1925, the general consensus of all involved was that the proceeding was winding down toward its finish. And the outcome of that finish seemed inevitable. The prosecution had not only shown beyond the shadow of a doubt that John Scopes had violated the Butler Act, but also managed to keep the defense from making its case that evolution was a universally accepted doctrine that should remain in the classroom. Assuming that for all intents and purposes the trial had ended on Friday, many of the press people had packed up their cameras and microphones and left over the weekend. This, as it turned out, was a move they would regret for the rest of their lives; for the real excitement of the Monkey Trial had yet to begin. The journalists who decided to stay on and cover Monday's session would have the distinction of witnessing and recording what the *New York Times* would later describe as "the most amazing court scene in Anglo-Saxon history."

"Read Your Evolution"?

The scene in court on Monday morning gave no hint of the gripping drama to come. Arthur Hays introduced still another argument about procedure. The judge had disallowed the defense's request to put its experts on the stand, to "offer proof," said Hays. But according to Tennessee law, an offer of proof could be introduced in two other ways, the first being a written statement, called an affidavit, which automatically entered the court record. The second way of offering proof was through an oral statement made by a defense counsel to the court. Opting for this method, Hays requested that he be allowed to read some of the scientific testimony out loud to the judge. Not surprisingly, the prosecution objected; but after giving the matter some thought, Judge Raulston granted the request. "I want to be fair to both sides," he said, "and it occurs to me that this is fair." And so, in the hour or so left before the lunch break, Hays went through the rather monotonous ritual of reading some of the witnesses' written statements.

When the court came back to order at about 1:30 P.M., Judge Raulston made an unexpected and disturbing announcement. He had been advised that cracks had appeared in the ceiling of the room below the court chamber, apparently the result of the

The main street of Dayton, Tennessee, is emptied of reporters who abandoned the town once the trial wound down and missed the trial's most exciting moments.

record-size crowds packing the hall day after day. Because of the danger of the floor collapsing, he said, court would have to reconvene on the front lawn. There, several minutes later, the judge and attorneys took their places on a raised platform usually used by preachers to deliver sermons, while over five thousand spectators gathered around under the blazing sun.

No sooner had everyone settled down when Clarence Darrow voiced an objection. He pointed to the courthouse wall, on which hung a huge sign bearing the slogan, "Read Your Bible." The sign might prejudice the jury against John Scopes and the defense, Darrow argued, and therefore it should be taken down immediately. The crowd clearly found this suggestion offensive, as did the prosecutors. Gordon McKenzie stood and shouted, "I have never seen the time in the history of this country when any man should be afraid to be reminded of the fact that he should read his Bible, and if they [the defense attorneys] should represent a force that is aligned with the devil and his satellites—" Before he could finish the thought, Dudley Malone was on his feet protesting that the defense had been unfairly maligned. The judge agreed and, while the court remained in an uproar with seemingly everyone talking at the same time, he ordered the phrase "devil and his satellites" stricken from the court record.

A Surprise Witness

The furor finally subsided when William Jennings Bryan stood up. Trying to act as a peacemaker, he quoted the apostle Paul's biblical line of reasoning, "If eating meat maketh my brother to offend, I shall eat no meat while the world lasts." Then, referring to the sign, Bryan added, "If leaving that up there during the trial makes our brother to offend, I would take it down during the trial." Darrow offered a compromise. The "Read Your Bible" sign could stay in place provided the defense be allowed to erect a banner the same size, bearing the message "Read Your Evolution," beside it. Without further ado, the judge ordered the offending sign removed. Then he recalled the jurors, who had not been allowed to hear either Hays's readings to the court or the arguments over the sign.

John Scopes, John Neal, and George Rappelyea walk in front of the "Read Your Bible" sign that Darrow insisted would influence the jury in favor of the prosecution.

At this juncture, Darrow played his ace. He signaled to Arthur Hays, who announced in a loud voice, "The defense desires to call Mr. Bryan as a witness." Everyone present was startled by this request, including Bryan himself, who suddenly increased the pace of his fanning. At first, the prosecution objected on the grounds that the defense's calling of the chief prosecutor as a witness was outlandish and unheard of. But the defense argued that such a tactic was perfectly legal; and besides, after having successfully blocked the introduction of expert testimony on evolution, why should the prosecutors fear expert testimony on the Bible? For Mr. Bryan was, after all, one of the country's leading biblical experts. Darrow later recalled:

The judge asked me if I considered it important. I reminded him that the [Butler] statute was based on a conflict between evolution and religion, and that we were entitled to prove the meaning of the words so that the jury could determine whether there was any conflict. Mr. Bryan relieved the situation by saying that he was perfectly willing to take the stand . . . on the condition that I would go [on the stand, too]. I said that they could put me on at any time they wished and I would try to answer their questions. And of course this left the judge with nothing to decide.

If the Earth Stood Still

Coatless and still waving his fan, Bryan crossed the platform and sat in the witness chair. Darrow approached his adversary, paused, and then began one of the most famous and fateful exchanges in trial history. "You have given considerable study to the Bible, haven't you, Mr. Bryan?"

"Yes, I have," the witness responded. "I have studied the Bible for about fifty years."

"Do you claim that everything in the Bible should be literally interpreted?" Darrow asked.

"I believe that everything in the Bible should be accepted as it is given there; some of the Bible is given illustratively. For instance: 'Ye are the salt of the earth.' I would not insist that man was actually salt, but it is used in the sense of salt as saving God's people."

Darrow then inquired how Bryan interpreted the story about Jonah being swallowed by a whale, and the Commoner affirmed his faith that God could make a person and a whale and make them both do whatever he pleased. Moving on to another well-known biblical story, Darrow asked, "Do you believe that Joshua made the sun stand still?"

"I believe what the Bible says," Bryan replied proudly.

Darrow raised an eyebrow. "I suppose you mean that the earth stood still?"

Clarence Darrow and William Jennings Bryan converse at the trial. Darrow shocked the courtroom when he exposed Bryan's ignorance on the witness stand.

"I don't know," Bryan answered. "I am talking about the Bible now. I accept the Bible absolutely."

"Do you believe at that time the entire sun went around the earth?"

"No, I believe the earth goes around the sun."

"Now, Mr. Bryan, have you ever pondered what would have happened to the earth if it stood still suddenly?"

"No." The witness tried to sound self-assured; but it was clear that such questions requiring scientific knowledge, which he sorely lacked, made him uncomfortable. Of course, this was exactly what Darrow wanted. His sole intention in putting his opponent on the stand had been to attempt to fluster Bryan, somehow to make him admit that his literal interpretation of the Bible might be too rigid and unreasonable.

Darrow suggested that if the earth had stopped, it would have been converted into a "molten mass." Then he began pressing Bryan about still another episode from the Bible. "Do you believe the story of the flood to be a literal interpretation?"

"Yes sir."

"When was the flood?"

"I would not attempt to fix the day," said Bryan, working his fan a little faster. Some of his admirers in the audience began to sense his nervousness.

"But what do you think the Bible itself says? Don't you know how it was arrived at?"

"I never made a calculation."

Darrow asked, "A calculation from what?"

"I could not say."

"From the generations of man?"

"I would not want to say that," Bryan replied curtly.

"What do you think?" Darrow demanded.

"I do not think about things I do not think about!" blurted the witness in an irritated tone.

"Do you think about things you *do* think about?" Darrow snapped back.

Seemingly confused, Bryan answered, "Well, sometimes." This statement drew laughter from some of the onlookers, including Judge Raulston. But for the first time since the start of the trial, people were laughing at, rather than with, the mighty orator. Many of his fans, shocked that he could appear so foolish and indecisive, stared with stunned and saddened expressions. The disconcerted Bryan sensed the change in the crowd and he turned and glared indignantly at some of the spectators.

9:00 A.M., October 23, 4004 B.C.

Having successfully lured his opponent into the trap, Darrow now pressed the questioning with renewed vigor. Again, the interrogator asked when the flood had taken place, and after some quick calculations Bryan replied, "Two thousand three hundred and forty-nine years B.C." The witness went on to explain that Bishop Ussher, a famous Bible scholar, had reckoned the date of God's creation of the world to the year 4004 B.C. In fact, said Bryan, the good bishop had even supplied the exact day and time—October 23 at 9:00 A.M. At this, an unknown person in the audience yelled out, "Eastern Standard Time!" Not used to such mockery, Bryan frowned.

Clarence Darrow (right) questions William Jennings Bryan during the Scopes trial. Darrow's probing questions left Bryan confused and humiliated.

Darrow then asked whether the witness believed that all the world's animal species had been created in 4004 B.C. and that only those on Noah's ark survived? "I think the fish may have lived," Bryan answered.

"Don't you know," inquired Darrow, "there are any number of civilizations that are traced back to more than five thousand years?"

"I am not satisfied by any evidence that I have seen."

"You have never had any interest in the age of the various races and peoples and civilizations and animals that exist upon the earth today?"

In a dismissive tone, Bryan replied, "I have never felt a great deal of interest in the effort that has been made to dispute the Bible by the speculations of men or the investigations of men."

"Don't you know," Darrow continued, "that the ancient civilizations of China are six thousand or seven thousand years old, at the very least?"

"No," said Bryan, adding adamantly, "but they would not run back beyond the creation, according to the Bible, six thousand years."

Who Begat Whom?

While on the witness stand, William Jennings Bryan found himself pressed to supply dates for both the biblical flood and the creation. Like most fundamentalists did at the time, he cited the dates calculated by the seventeenth-century Irish theologian James Ussher. Ussher became a priest in 1601, a bishop in 1621, and the archbishop of Armagh in 1625. Like other theologians of his time, he believed implicitly in the Bible's historical accuracy; therefore, he reasoned, it should be possible to calculate the actual dates of historical events mentioned in the Old Testament. To this end, the archbishop carefully studied the biblical texts, taking note of the genealogies, or records of ancestors and their descendants, including who "begat" whom and the lengths of the generations of many biblical patriarchs, judges, priests, and kings. Working ever backward in time, Ussher finally concluded that the great flood had occurred in 2349 B.C. and the creation in 4004 B.C. He published these conclusions in 1650, and for many years his chronology was printed in the margins of most of the English-language versions of the Bible. It is interesting to note that Bryan was incorrect in stating that Ussher had arrived at an exact dating of October 23 (a Sunday, of course) at 9:00 for the creation. This calculation was contributed by the noted English scholar, John Lightfoot, a few years after Ussher published his own work.

"You don't know how old they are; is that right?"

"I don't know how old they are," the Commoner admitted, "but probably you do. I think you would give the preference to anybody who opposed the Bible."

Darrow smiled and said, "Well, you are welcome to your opinion. Have you any idea how old the Egyptian civilization is?"

"No."

"Mr. Bryan, you don't know whether any other religion ever gave a similar account of the destruction of the earth by the flood?"

"The Christian religion has satisfied me," Bryan declared proudly, "and I have never felt it necessary to look up some competing religions."

"Do you know how old the Confucian religion is?"

"I can't give you the exact date of it."

"Do you know how old the religion of Zoroaster [an ancient Persian prophet] is?"

"No sir."

"What about the religion of Confucius or Buddha? Do you regard them as competitive?"

"No, I think they are very inferior. Would you like for me to tell you what I know about it?"

"No," said Darrow. "Do you know anything about how many people there were in Egypt thirty-five hundred years ago or how many people there were in China five thousand years ago?"

"No."

"Have you ever tried to find out?"

"No sir; you are the first man I ever heard of that has been interested in it." Under Darrow's relentless and skillful stream of questions, Bryan had revealed his nearly complete ignorance of world history. But what even some of Bryan's supporters now saw as the pathetic spectacle of his undoing did not end there. Darrow kept at his task minute after grueling minute under the searing summer sun, steadily chipping away at Bryan's once majestic image.

The Length of a Biblical Day

After more than an hour on the stand, Bryan showed not only that he was ignorant of history, but that he knew practically nothing of the established and universally accepted facts of archaeology, geology, astronomy, and other scholarly disciplines. The man who had so vigorously advocated limiting the teaching of science in the schools had just demonstrated that he had not the foggiest notion of what science was all about. The reactions from the crowd were mixed. Those few who had long maintained that Bryan was shallow and ignorant felt vindicated. Among his far more numerous supporters, some looked befuddled and many others seemed to feel sorry for him; but most were at least thankful for his continued unflagging defense of God and a literal interpretation of the Bible.

But then Bryan said something that even many of his staunchest advocates saw as a betrayal of the fundamentalist cause. Seeing that his opponent was now clearly tired, listless, nervous, and confused, Darrow returned to the subject of the Bible. "Do you think the earth was made in six days?" he asked.

"Not six days of twenty-four hours," Bryan answered. At the sound of these six fateful words, shocked gasps came from various sections of the crowd. "What does he want to say that for?" someone in the rear of the throng demanded. At the heart of the fundamentalist doctrine lies the belief that every word in the Bible was a truth to be accepted ex-

Although it became obvious that Darrow was besting Bryan, Bryan refused to give up, continuing to testify until he made several major blunders.

actly as stated, so that when the Book of Genesis said that God had shaped the earth in six days, it meant six ordinary days, *days of twenty-four hours*. Yet the great champion of biblical literalists everywhere had just denied this "holy truth."

Darrow immediately realized the import of his opponent's unfortunate remark and pounced on the opportunity. Sounding astonished, the chief defense attorney asked, "Doesn't the Bible say so?"

"No sir," Bryan repeated, eliciting more gasps from the audience.

Prosecutor Stewart realized that his colleague was in serious trouble and attempted to rescue him. "What is the purpose of this examination?" Stewart demanded, leaping to his feet.

But before either Darrow or the judge could answer, Bryan answered for them. "The purpose is to cast ridicule on everybody who believes in the Bible!" the witness said in a loud and angry voice.

Darrow answered this charge with equal gruffness. "We have the purpose of preventing bigots and ignoramuses from controlling the education of the United States and you know it—and that is all!"

Evening and Morning Without Sun?

At this point a lengthy argument erupted among the prosecutors, defense lawyers, and the judge. Dudley Malone charged that Bryan was trying to get biblical "evidence" into the court record to distort or disprove the scientists' statements that Hays had earlier read aloud. After Bryan angrily denied this, Stewart again tried to convince Judge Raulston to terminate the interrogation of Bryan. Raulston agreed with Stewart that the questions Darrow had been asking were not proper testimony for a jury but said that he would permit them for the record. This greatly pleased the defense because any and all statements in the record could be used later, if Scopes were found guilty, to open up and conduct an appeal to a higher court. Upset and indignant, Bryan wanted to make it clear to all present that he had not taken the

Clarence Darrow's grueling questioning of William Jennings Bryan was the centerpiece of the trial.

stand to aid some future defense appeal. "I want the Christian world to know," he bellowed, "that any atheist, agnostic, unbeliever, can question me any time as to my belief in God, and I will answer him!"

And so, Darrow's questioning of Bryan continued. Darrow shrewdly continued to emphasize the witness's uncertainty and flexibility about the length of a biblical day. The defender read aloud that passage from Genesis that states, "The morning and the evening were the first day." Then he turned to Bryan and asked, "Do you think the sun was made on the fourth day?"

"Yes."

"And they had evening and morning without the sun?"

"I am simply saying it is a period," corrected Bryan. He seemed to be digging himself in ever deeper and Darrow took advantage of it by asking if by a "period" he meant that the creation might have lasted a long time, perhaps longer than six ordinary days? The creation "might have continued for millions of years," Bryan admitted. Still more gasps came from the audience. Many of the onlookers were just plain mad at Bryan for his apparent heresy against fundamentalist doctrine; but at least a few people began to realize that if a biblical day was actually millions of years long, then the earth might be as old as the evolutionists and geologists claimed. God might have created the world and then given plants and animals plenty of time to change and develop, in which case religion and evolution might be reconciled after all; and if so, what was all the fuss about?

Darrow continued the grilling until the exhausted and flustered Bryan, on hearing another derisive laugh from the crowd, lost whatever composure he had left. In an emotional outburst, the Great Commoner told the judge, "Your honor, I think I can shorten this testimony. The only purpose Mr. Darrow has is to slur at the Bible, but I will answer his questions, I shall answer them at once. I want the world to know that this man, who does not believe in a God, is trying to use a court in Tennessee—"

"I object to your statement," Darrow interrupted loudly. "I am examining you on your fool ideas that no intelligent Christian on earth believes!"

Dudley Malone, John T. Scopes, and Clarence Darrow pose for the camera.

Triumph and Tragedy

And then it was suddenly over. Distressed that the questioning had degenerated into little more than a shouting match, Judge Raulston ended the interrogation, excused Bryan, and adjourned court for the day. For the two giants who had just clashed, it was a moment of triumph for one and tragedy for the other. Hundreds of people pressed in to congratulate Darrow, most of them passing by and ignoring the crestfallen Bryan. Darrow later recalled:

Much to my surprise, the great gathering began to surge toward me. They seemed to have changed sides in a single afternoon. A friendly crowd followed me toward my home. Mr. Bryan left the grounds practically alone. The people seemed to feel that he had failed and deserted his cause and his followers when he admitted that the first six days might have been periods of millions of ages long. Mr. Bryan had made himself ridiculous and had contradicted his own faith. I was truly sorry for Mr. Bryan. But I consoled myself by thinking of the years through which he had busied himself tormenting intelligent professors with impudent questions about their faith, and seeking to arouse the ignoramuses and bigots to drive them out of their [teaching] positions.

To many it seemed as if Darrow had won a conclusive victory that day. But the reality was that the Scopes trial was not yet over, and neither was the controversy that had inspired it.

Chapter 6

A Still-Smoldering
Controversy: The
Legacy of the
Scopes Trial

IN THE EVENING OF JULY 20, 1925, only hours after the devastating confrontation between Darrow and Bryan in Dayton, late newspaper editions across the country carried stories and editorials about the showdown. The vast majority were very critical of Bryan and his support for efforts to change and censor school curricula. Typical were the comments made by the great American humorist Will Rogers in his popular syndicated newspaper column:

> Now personally, I like Bill [Bryan], but when he says that he will make this his life's issue and take it up through all the various courts and finally get it into the Constitution of the United States . . . he is wrong. More wrong than he has ever been before. These other things he was wrong on [in his testimony] didn't do much harm, but now he is going to try to drag . . . the Bible into a political campaign. He can't ever do that. He might make Tennessee the side show of America, but he can't make a street carnival of the whole United States.

But though Bryan had taken a beating at the hands of Darrow and the press that day, the next day it was the turn of Darrow and

Scopes's other attorneys to suffer a setback. When court reconvened on the morning of Tuesday, July 21, Judge Raulston ruled that Bryan could not go back on the stand. What is more, all Bryan's testimony from the preceding session had to be stricken from the court record. This was a definite blow to the defense because it had no further means of presenting its position on the issue of evolution versus the Bible. The Scopes trial was over and nothing remained but for the jury to render its verdict.

The Verdict and Closing Statements

After the judge summoned the jury that morning, Darrow asked that he might address the panel. Darrow was worried that the jurors might find Scopes not guilty, in which case the defense would lose its right to appeal the case to a higher court and the Butler Act would remain on the books. The efforts of Darrow, the ACLU, and the others to stop the campaign against the teaching of evolution in American schools would come to noth-

Clarence Darrow (leaning against desk) found himself in the unusual position of insisting his client was guilty.

ing. For this reason, Darrow emphasized to the jury that Scopes had broken the law and that they had no other choice but to find him guilty; and Judge Raulston also gave the jurors instructions to the same effect.

The jury then promptly did its duty and delivered a guilty verdict. Since the Butler Act provided for a minimum penalty of $100, the judge sentenced John Scopes to pay a fine in that amount. A few seconds later, all eyes in the courtroom focused on the former teacher, who, wearing a white shirt and a bow tie, stood before the judge's bench to make the closing statement the law allowed him. "Your honor," he began,

John T. Scopes listens as he is sentenced for teaching evolution in violation of the Butler Act.

I feel that I have been convicted of violating an unjust statute. I will continue in the future as I have in the past, to oppose this law in any way I can. Any other action would be in violation of my ideal of academic freedom— that is, to teach the truth as guaranteed in our constitution, of personal and religious freedom. I think the fine is unjust.

Next, Arthur Hays made the official request that the court permit the defense to appeal the case and the judge granted it without discussion. After several of the attorneys, including Darrow and Bryan, made short closing statements, Judge Raulston made his own, the fair and noble tone of which impressed Darrow greatly. The judge did not name Scopes specifically, but there could be little doubt that the speech was aimed at the man who had just been found guilty. "It sometimes takes courage," Raulston declared,

> to search diligently for a truth that may destroy our pre-conceived notions and ideas. It sometimes takes courage to declare a truth or stand for an act that is in contravention to [goes against] the public sentiment. A man who is big enough to search for the truth and find it and declare it in the face of all opposition is a big man.

With these words, what nearly everyone in the world at that time perceived as the "trial of the century" officially ended.

The Trial's Immediate Aftermath

Over too was the Dayton carnival. The Bible sellers and hot dog vendors packed up and left, and the tents and banners of the revivalists came down, so that within a few days the town's main squares gave little or no hint that they had so recently harbored a world-class event. After the transformation, a Knoxville journalist reported: "A lonesome quietness seemed to hover over the little Tennessee village. The only visitors to the courthouse were now and then some who had attended the trial and left some of their belongings in the courtroom."

One important visitor stayed on in Dayton, however. William Jennings Bryan, his once gleaming reputation now tarnished, remained in hopes of delivering a long oration he had not been allowed to present on the last morning of the trial. Five days after the judge's gavel had closed the proceeding, Bryan, following his personal habit, ate a huge afternoon meal and then lay down to take a nap. This time he never woke up. On hearing the news of his passing, some of his remaining supporters proposed that after his terrible humiliation on the witness stand he had "died of a broken heart," while Darrow was quoted as saying, "Broken heart nothing; he died of a busted belly." The actual medical diagnosis was stroke, probably related to Bryan's diabetes.

Thus, Bryan did not live to see the results of the appeal, which Darrow and the other defense attorneys brought to the Tennessee Supreme Court almost a year later. Of the four justices who heard the case, two ended up declaring the Butler Act constitutional; one ruled that the law was constitutional but that Scopes had not actually violated it; and the remaining justice decided that the statute was unconstitutional. With a three-to-one vote upholding its legality, the Butler Act remained on Tennessee's books. There was an ironic footnote, however. On a technicality, the justices overruled Judge Raulston's sentence and revoked Scopes's $100 fine.

Scopes himself, who had never felt comfortable in the public limelight, then returned to an obscure private life, although he never again taught high school; after attending the University of Chicago, he thereafter made his living as a geologist. As for Clarence Darrow, he moved on to more controversial cases, including one involving the revenge murder of an accused rapist. He published a widely read autobiography in 1932 and died in Chicago in 1938 at the age of eighty. After that, he and his chief opponent in the Scopes trial, William Jennings Bryan, developed images even more legendary than they had enjoyed in life. Now a part of American folklore, their characters still argue about the length of a biblical day in countless stage productions, as well as the film version, of *Inherit the Wind*, the drama based on the infamous eight-day Dayton Monkey Trial.

Darwin Under the Desk

The legacy of the Scopes trial itself, in the sense of who ultimately won and lost, has been mixed. On the one hand, Darrow's side—the cause of science and academic freedom—benefited greatly over time, even though the Tennessee high court upheld the validity of the Butler Act. A similar law passed in Mississippi in 1926; however, that same year the Kentucky and Louisiana legislatures rejected antievolution bills. The press, as well as scientists and academic spokespersons across the nation, continued to depict those who advocated such laws as backward and ignorant. In the wake of what seemed to be a

moral victory for Scopes and his defenders and supporters, the
fundamentalist drive to censor science in the schools steadily
lost steam. By the 1940s, the conflict between evolution and the
Bible had become a largely forgotten issue. And in the 1960s, the
U.S. Supreme Court finally overturned the Butler Act (and the
few remaining antievolution laws in other states) by ruling that
the teaching of evolution is constitutional.

On the other hand, the fundamentalists won what might be
termed a silent victory. Even though the campaign to ban the
work of Darwin from the public schools had been more or less
discredited, many southern teachers, school administrators, and
textbook publishers remained anxious and fearful about teaching evolution. For almost thirty-five years after the Scopes trial,
only a handful of high school biology texts in the country
retained sections on Darwin and evolution; and most high school
biology teachers either mentioned the topic only briefly or
skipped it altogether.

A cartoon from an 1861 issue of
Punch *pokes fun at the evolution*
controversy.

MONKEYANA.

AM I
A
MAN AND
A
BROTHER?

AM I satyr or man?
Pray tell me who can,
And settle my place in the scale.
A man in ape's shape,
An anthropoid ape,
Or monkey deprived of his tail?

A few enterprising teach-
ers did manage to slip Darwin into the curriculum
"through the back door." In
some Tennessee towns, for
example, instructors men-
tioned Darwin and his
famous book in literature
classes, since by discussing
its literary merits they were
technically not "teaching
the theory that man has
descended from a lower
order of animals," as forbid-
den in the Butler Act. Yet in
the same towns, librarians
usually kept their copies of
the *Origin of Species* under
the front desk and loaned
them out by special request

only. Not until the Soviet launch of the satellite *Sputnik I* in 1957 had jolted the United States into a feverish campaign to promote science education did most school textbooks and biology classes once more routinely devote time to evolution, as they had before the mid-1920s.

The Rise of Creationism

But with Darwin's return to the classroom came a new surge of fundamentalist concern about children being exposed to a doctrine that seemed to contradict the biblical story of creation. By the late 1960s, the number of fundamentalists in the United States had grown to an estimated fifty million. Many, like their predecessors in Dayton, Tennessee, wanted to see evolution excluded from classrooms; but with laws like the Butler Act now ruled unconstitutional, that was no longer possible. There was also no way to teach the Bible in public schools because that violated the First Amendment's intent with respect to separation of church and state. To get around these obstacles, as scholar Michael Ruse explains, some hard-core fundamentalists changed their approach and in the process redefined themselves:

> They would like to exclude evolution, but they cannot. They would like to include Genesis, but they cannot. As a compromise, therefore, they try to slide Genesis into classrooms, sideways. They argue that . . . all of the claims of Genesis can be supported by the best principles and premises of empirical science. In other words, *as scientists*, people can argue for instant creation of the universe, separate ancestry for man and apes, short time span for the earth (between approximately 6,000 and 20,000 years), and a universal flood over everything, at some later date. Hence, we have the growth of "Scientific Creationism" or "Creation Science."

All through the 1970s, the creationists lobbied for "equal time" and "balanced treatment" in classrooms, arguing that evolution was only "one of the theories" for human origins. The biblical creation was another and equally worthy theory, they insisted, and should therefore be taught right alongside evolution in biology classes. These efforts were unsuccessful until 1981 when a bill, titled Act 590, came before the Arkansas legislature. Act 590 provided that, if human origins were discussed in a public classroom, the teacher must cover "Creation-science" along with "Evolution-science." On March 19 of that same year Governor Frank J. White signed the bill into law.

Immediately, many groups and individuals came out against the new law. Among them were several southern clergymen, who felt that religion was the province of churches, not schools, and also many local business organizations, which feared that a blow to science education might discourage lucrative high-tech companies from migrating to Arkansas. With the aid of the ACLU, which had been instrumental in the Scopes case, they challenged Act 590 on the grounds that it violated the doctrine of separation of church and state, that it infringed on teachers' "academic freedom," and that the law was vague from a legal standpoint.

These arguments against Act 590 eventually won out. On January 5, 1982, the judge hearing the case ruled that "Creation-science" was religion, not science, and could not be taught in public classrooms. The state of Arkansas did not appeal the decision. Later, in 1987, the U.S. Supreme Court made an almost identical ruling that struck down a pro-creationist act that had recently passed in Louisiana.

A Grand View of Life

But despite these setbacks, advocates of creationism remained active. In the 1990s, as they continued their efforts to gain equal time with evolutionists, some conservative politicians aided them with supportive public statements. Early in 1996, Republican presidential hopeful Pat Buchanan told an ABC reporter, "I believe you're a creature of God. I think [parents] have a right to insist that Godless evolution not be taught to their children or their children not be indoctrinated in it." Encouraged by such support, politically active creationists worked to chip away at what they saw as an unfair evolutionist stranglehold on education. In March 1996, the Tennessee legislature considered a bill

THE SUPERNATURAL VERSUS THE TESTABLE

In the 1981 court case known as *McLean v. Arkansas*, in which the state's Act 590 underwent a legal challenge, Michael Ruse, a professor at the University of Guelph, Ontario, and the author of *The Darwinian Revolution* (1978), testified as an expert scientific witness. In the following excerpt from the court record, Ruse explains why he thinks creation science does not "measure up to the standards and characteristics" of real science:

> In my opinion creation science does not have those attributes that distinguish science from other endeavors. . . . First and most importantly, creation science necessarily looks to the supernatural acts of a Creator. . . . Moreover, because the supernatural forces are the acts of a Creator, that is, the acts of a God, they are not subject to scientific investigation or understanding. This nonscientific aspect of creation science emerges quite clearly from the creation-science literature I have read. . . . Let me give you an example in the evolution/creation controversy. The example pertains to homologies. Homologies are structural similarities between different organisms of widely different species. For example . . . the wing of a bat and the arm of a man are strikingly similar. These similarities cannot be explained by function: obviously, a man's arm and a bat's wing have different functions. Evolutionary theory gives an explanation for homologies. This explanation is: Organisms with homologies are descended from common ancestors. Creationism, on the other hand, does not give any explanation for homologies. The theory of creation is that a Creator created a bat's wing and man's arm independently. But that theory does not give any explanation of why they are similar. . . . Creation science is neither testable nor tentative. Indeed, an attribute of creation science that distinguishes it quite clearly from science is that it is absolutely certain about all of the answers. And considering the magnitude of the questions it addresses—the origins of man, life, the earth, and the universe—that certainty is all the more revealing. Whatever the contrary evidence, creation science never accepts that its theory is falsified. This is just the opposite of tentativeness and makes a mockery of testing.

that would require school boards to dismiss teachers who present evolution as scientific fact. And in Alabama, creationists successfully pushed to get biology textbooks to include a disclaimer saying that evolution is a "controversial theory" that only "some

The teaching of Charles Darwin's theories in public schools is still challenged by fundamentalist Christians today.

scientists" accept. (Opponents say this statement is ludicrous, pointing out that virtually all reputable scientists accept evolution.)

Thus, the controversy that Charles Darwin ignited in 1859, which flared up again in the 1925 Scopes trial, continues to smolder. Darwin himself would, no doubt, be perplexed at the longevity of these arguments, for he easily reconciled the concept of God with that of evolution. "To my mind," he wrote in the moving finale of the *Origin of Species*, "it accords better with what we know of the laws impressed on matter by the Creator, that the production and extinction of the past and present inhabitants of the world should have been due to secondary causes." Because modern animals and people could trace their lineage back for hundreds of millions of years, he said, it was obvious that no catastrophe had ever managed to destroy the thread of life; and this showed that God's design of natural selection assured that life would survive far into the future. Finally, Darwin suggested that God's conception of a process as fantastically complex, productive, and durable as evolution was far more awesome than that of a sudden and simple miraculous creation. "There is grandeur in this view of life," he stated, describing evolution,

> having been originally breathed by the Creator into a few forms or into one; and that, whilst this planet has gone cycling on according to the fixed law of gravity, from so simple a beginning endless forms most beautiful and most wonderful have been, and are being evolved.

For Further Reading

L. Sprague de Camp, *The Great Monkey Trial*. Garden City, NY: Doubleday, 1968. Like de Camp's other books, for instance the classic *Ancient Engineers*, this study of the Scopes trial is thoroughly researched and documented, clearly written, and highly entertaining.

L. Sprague de Camp and Catherine C. de Camp, *Darwin and His Great Discovery*. New York: Macmillan, 1972. Another excellent de Camp volume, this one explaining the intricacies of evolutionary theory in very understandable language.

John E. Driemen, *Clarence Darrow*. New York: Chelsea House, 1992. A clearly written general synopsis of Darrow's life and his most important and famous court cases.

Walter Karp, *Charles Darwin and the Origin of Species*. New York: American Heritage, 1968. A well-written overview of Darwin's thesis about the evolution of higher life-forms from lower ones, including sections about the controversy the book originally generated.

Jerome Lawrence and Robert E. Lee, *Inherit the Wind*. Originally produced on Broadway in 1955. Reprinted. New York: Bantam Books, 1982. This is the intellectually stimulating and highly entertaining play based on the Scopes trial. The authors have changed the names of Bryan, Darrow, Scopes, and other main characters but have retained the essence of the proceeding, including close paraphrases of many of the lines from the actual court transcripts. I also strongly recommend the 1960 film version of *Inherit the Wind*, directed by Stanley Kramer and starring Spencer Tracy and Fredric March (available on videotape). Tracy and March, two of the greatest American film actors of the century, deliver spectacular performances in the Darrow and Bryan roles respectively, and the whole film is gripping throughout. The 1988 TV version, with Kirk Douglas in the Bryan role, is adequate but does not compare to the earlier movie.

89

Tom McGowen, *The Great Monkey Trial: Science vs. Fundamentalism in America*. New York: Franklin Watts, 1990. This very
thorough and well-written overview of the trial also contains
useful information about the backgrounds of Bryan, Darrow,
and the other major participants, as well as about how fundamentalism grew in America.

Don Nardo, *Charles Darwin*. New York: Chelsea House, 1993. A
detailed but easy-to-read overview of Darwin's life, including
his early interest in nature, the famous voyage of the HMS
Beagle, in which he gathered evidence that would later but-
tress his evolution theory, how that theory developed, the
writing of the *Origin of Species*, the controversy following the
book's publication, and Darwin's later writings and endeavors.

Works Consulted

Leslie H. Allen, ed., *Bryan and Darrow at Dayton: The Records and Documents of the Bible-Evolution Trial.* New York: Arthur Lee, 1925.

Robert W. Cherny, *A Righteous Cause: The Life of William Jennings Bryan.* Boston: Little, Brown, 1985.

Clarence Darrow, *The Story of My Life.* New York: Charles Scribner's Sons, 1932.

Charles Darwin, *On the Origin of Species By Means of Natural Selection or the Preservation of Favored Races in the Struggle for Life.* First published in England in 1859. New York: New American Library, 1958.

Ray Ginger, *Six Days or Forever?: Tennessee v. John Thomas Scopes.* New York: Oxford University Press, 1958.

Robert M. Hazen and James Trefil, *Science Matters: Achieving Scientific Literacy.* Garden City, NY: Doubleday, 1991.

The Holy Bible (Revised Standard Version). New York: Thomas Nelson and Sons, 1952.

Michael Ruse, *But Is It Science?: The Philosphical Question in the Creation/Evolution Controversy.* Buffalo, NY: Prometheus Press, 1988.

Irving Stone, *Clarence Darrow for the Defense.* Garden City, NY: Doubleday, 1941.

Arthur Weinberg, *Attorney for the Damned.* New York: Simon and Schuster, 1983.

Index

Picture Credits

Cover photo: The Bettmann Archive

AP/Wide World Photos, 29, 31, 45 (top), 52

Archive Photos, 9, 11, 21, 22, 34, 40, 48, 60, 64, 70, 72, 75

Archive Photos/American Stock, 50

Archive Photos/Hirz, 66

The Bettmann Archive, 15, 30, 32

Bettmann/Hulton, 19 (bottom), 84, 88

Corbis-Bettmann, 14, 19 (top), 39, 68, 80

Hulton Deutsch Collection Limited, 61

North Wind Picture Archives, 24

UPI/Bettmann Newsphotos, 36, 76, 78

UPI/Corbis-Bettmann, 42, 44, 45 (bottom), 46, 51, 55, 56, 57, 63, 81

About the Author

Don Nardo has written more than seventy books on a wide variety of topics. In addition to *The Trial of Socrates*, and *The Trial of Joan of Arc*, also for this trials series, his works include biographies of Charles Darwin, Thomas Jefferson, Franklin D. Roosevelt, H. G. Wells, Jim Thorpe, Joseph Smith, John Wayne, Julius Caesar, and Cleopatra. A classical historian by specialty, he has written many volumes about ancient Greece and Rome, among them *Greek and Roman Theater*, *Life in Ancient Greece*, *Life in Ancient Rome*, *The Battle of Marathon*, *Philip and Alexander: The Unification of Greece*, and *Caesar's Conquest of Gaul*. Mr. Nardo lives with his wife, Christine, on Cape Cod, Massachusetts.